MW00529290

YOU ARE THE HAPPINESS YOU SEEK

You Are the Happiness You Seek

Uncovering the Awareness of Being

RUPERT SPIRA

SAHAJA

newharbinger
publications

SAHAJA PUBLICATIONS

PO Box 887, Oxford OX1 9PR
www.sahajapublications.com

A co-publication with New Harbinger Publications
5674 Shattuck Ave.
Oakland, CA 94609
United States of America

Distributed in Canada by Raincoast Books

Copyright © Rupert Spira 2022
All rights reserved

No part of this book shall be reproduced or transmitted
in any form or by any means, electronic or mechanical, including
photocopying, recording, or by any information retrieval system
without written permission of the publisher

Designed by Rob Bowden

Printed in U.S.A.
ISBN 978-1-68403-012-5

Library of Congress Cataloging-in-Publication Data on file with publisher

Printed on paper made from wood sourced from
responsibly managed forests and recycled materials

To be open to the source of all happiness is the highest religion.

J. KRISHNAMURTI

CONTENTS

ACKNOWLEDGEMENTS

I would like to thank all those who have helped with the editing, designing and publishing of this book, including all those who have attended my meetings in person or online, the responses to whose questions are woven into its pages.

In particular, I would like to thank Caroline Seymour, Jacqueline Boyle, Bridget Holding and Lynne Saner for their editorial work, and Rob Bowden for preparing the manuscript for publication.

I would like to thank Ruth Middleton and Francesca Rotondella, without whose support in the background I'm not sure this book would have ever emerged, and Stuart Moore and Tom Tarbert for their generosity and kindness. I would also like to thank everyone at New Harbinger Publications for their continued help and support.

A Silent Prayer

And the end of all our exploring
Will be to arrive where we started
And know the place for the first time.

T. S. ELIOT

It is mid-afternoon on the 20th of March 2020, and a silent, invisible intruder has brought humanity to a standstill. Almost overnight I have cancelled all live speaking engagements for the foreseeable future and have transferred my activities online. My first online retreat, with five hundred people from around the world, will shortly begin.

When holding a meeting or retreat, I do not plan what I am going to say. I often sit quietly in an attitude of unarticulated prayer that my understanding, such as it is, might formulate itself in response to the moment. And this is no ordinary moment.

I check my emails, and my attention is attracted to one whose subject is *World Happiness Day*. A friend has sent me a message letting me know that today, the Spring Equinox, has, since 2006, been designated by the UN an international day of happiness, in honour of the understanding that 'the happiness, well-being and freedom of all life on earth is the ultimate purpose of every human being, nation, and society'.*

How poignant and how ironic, when the world finds itself plunged into a crisis which will bring untold distress and hardship to so many people, that this day should be consecrated a day of happiness, well-being and freedom.

The familiar objects, activities and relationships that we take for granted are rapidly being removed from us: the freedom to earn a living, to socialise and to travel, a plentiful supply of food and goods in shops, education for our children and grandchildren, and security for our future.

* See https://www.dayofhappiness.net.

But what about happiness? Can it be given and withdrawn? If so, by whom or what? What is its cause? Is it something that is taken in from the outside, or does it originate within us? Is there such a thing as lasting peace and happiness, or is this destined to alternate with suffering for the rest of our lives?

These questions have troubled the minds of innumerable people for thousands of years, and as I ponder them I recall the first time they formulated themselves in my mind. It was 1980 and I was twenty years old, living on the edge of Bodmin Moor in Cornwall in the South West of England, studying pottery with Michael Cardew, then eighty years old and one of the founders of the British Studio Pottery movement.

It was a somewhat monastic existence, and in many ways life at Wenford Bridge – Michael's home and pottery – resembled an apprenticeship with an old Zen master. However, I had a friend, and, although we rarely saw each other due to the remoteness of my circumstance, her presence in my life was a source of consolation and happiness.

Every Friday evening after dinner, I would walk a mile or so up the hill to the phone box on the edge of the village of St. Breward, beneath which the pottery was situated, and call my companion. It was something of a ritual whose anticipation and memory, as much as the event itself, sustained me throughout the week.

On this occasion, the quality of her first 'Hello' conveyed everything I needed to know. The brief conversation that ensued simply confirmed it. Little did I know then that her parting words were to be one of life's great gifts to me.

Later that night, lying awake in bed, as the initial wave of confusion and sorrow began to subside, I kept asking myself how a person can be the source of happiness one moment and the source of misery the next. For the first time in my life, I became acutely aware of the extent to which I had invested my happiness in my circumstances, in this case in a relationship.

I had already been interested in spiritual matters for some time, and since my mid-teens had been studying philosophy and practising meditation in the Vedantic and Sufi traditions at Colet House in London, under the guidance of Dr. Francis Roles. However, this event injected intensity and urgency into my interest; it became a passion.

It was obvious that I loved happiness above all else. It was also clear that nothing objective is certain or secure, and clearly does not unfold according to one's own wishes and expectations. And now the absurdity and futility of investing one's desire for lasting happiness in objective experience was inescapable. I fell asleep that night with a simple question in my mind, 'How may one find lasting peace and happiness?'

Almost exactly forty years later, circumstances are again demanding this question be addressed. However, on this occasion it is not just my personal circumstances that have precipitated the question in my mind, nor is it individual happiness that is at stake. It is the shared circumstances of each one of us that requires a response, and our collective happiness that is calling for attention.

The universe had responded to my silent prayer. Our online retreat began with this question, and the exploration of it evolved into this book. It is my hope that this book will take you from your self, who seeks happiness, to the happiness that is your self.

Rupert Spira
April 2021

CHAPTER ONE

The Search for Happiness

Happiness, being found to be something final and
self-sufficient, is the end at which all actions aim.

ARISTOTLE

WE SEEK HAPPINESS ABOVE ALL ELSE

Imagine a survey in which all seven billion of us were asked what we want
in life above all else. Most of us would respond that we desire better health,
increased income, an intimate relationship, improved living conditions,
a family, better work or preferably no need to work at all, and so on. Some
of us would ask for less tangible things: enlightenment or knowledge of God.
Whatever our priorities, most of us would select from a relatively short list
of possibilities.

However, if a second question then asked *why* we desire what we do,
almost all of us would respond, in one way or another, that we seek the
object, substance, activity, circumstance or relationship because we believe
it will bring us peace and happiness.

In other words, what we really long for is not a particular experience for its
own sake, but for the peace and happiness that we believe we will derive from it.
If we knew that the house we were about to buy, the person we were about
to marry, the journey we were about to embark on or the job we were about
to begin would make us miserable, we would no longer want it. We wish for
these things only insofar as they are considered a source of happiness.

Even those who voluntarily undergo great hardship for the sake of
a moral, political, religious or spiritual ideal do so ultimately for the sake
of happiness, even if, in extreme cases, that happiness is postponed until
after death.

The desire for happiness is, therefore, the driving force in most of
our lives.

This longing for happiness takes us on a great adventure in the realm of objective experience. By 'objective experience' I do not refer to physical objects alone but to any experience that has some kind of form, including all thoughts, images, feelings, sensations, perceptions, activities and relationships.

Although any of these may seem to afford moments or periods of happiness, sooner or later they come to an end, the old dissatisfaction resurfaces and the search begins again.

Once the search in the conventional realm of objective experience has failed to deliver lasting happiness sufficiently often, many people turn to a religious or spiritual tradition. In this case, the goal, however we may conceive it, is the same: peace, joy, fulfilment, contentment or wholeness. Only the means have changed. Even those of us who seek enlightenment on a spiritual path, or God on a religious path, do so only on account of the peace and happiness we believe we will derive from it.

If someone were to ask us whether we would prefer to be enlightened or happy, we would obviously choose happiness. If we believed that enlightenment would bring us misery, we would never seek it. It is only because it is believed that enlightenment will bring happiness that we are willing to devote our lives to seeking it. Likewise, if we believed that knowledge of God would make us miserable, no one would seek God.

The only reason we were seeking enlightenment or God in the first place was that all other possible sources of happiness had failed us thus far. It is often as a last resort that we turn to the search for enlightenment or God, in the hope that its fulfilment will finally relieve us of our suffering and provide happiness.

Therefore, the desire for happiness is the highest desire, and as such it is unique: it is the only thing we seek for its own sake.

I use the word 'happiness' as the goal of this search simply because it is the common word for the absence of suffering or the end of seeking. I refer to it this way because I believe, rightly or not, that this word most accurately conveys for the majority of people that for which they long above all else. It is also a word to which everyone can relate, and it refers to an experience with which everyone is familiar. In particular, it is non-denominational and devoid of cultural overtones. It does not have to be believed in and is its own evidence.

However, any word inevitably has its limitations, depending upon our particular associations with it, especially in relation to that for which we all long above all else. If the word 'happiness' does not evoke in you that which you love and for which you long above all else, please substitute it with another: fulfilment, contentment, peace, love, truth, beauty, joy, salvation, liberation, enlightenment or God.

Whether we feel a strong yearning in our heart or just the slightest sense of dissatisfaction – the feeling that something is missing which, when found, will finally bring about the happiness for which we long – we are on a great search. However we conceive or name the goal of that search, its source is always the same, namely, the desire to bring our current dissatisfaction to an end.

If happiness is what we all love and long for above all else, then the investigation into its nature and cause must be the greatest endeavour on which one could embark.

HAPPINESS IS INHERENT WITHIN US

Happiness is always experienced inside us; it is never put in from the outside. It may seem to be connected to or triggered by external events, but unlike the food we eat, the water we drink or the air we breathe, we do not take it into ourself from outside. It originates within us, it is experienced within us and, when it disappears, no residue of it is dispersed into the outside world. Happiness is entirely an interior experience.

If happiness is always experienced within, albeit triggered by objective experience, mustn't it lie in potential in us all the time? And if so, shouldn't it be possible to have direct access to it, and to remain constantly in touch with it, without the need for our external circumstances to be configured in a particular way?

If it *were* possible to be in touch with our inherent peace and happiness without being dependent on external circumstances, would that not be the greatest discovery one could make?

One might argue that *unhappiness* is also always experienced inside us and must, therefore, lie latent within us at all times. According to this view, our inherent happiness or unhappiness would simply be triggered by circumstances, depending on the extent to which they conform to our desire or expectation.

Although most people may not formulate it to themselves in this way, this is the common view of happiness and suffering. They are considered equal and opposite emotions, alternating in varying degrees in our lives, depending upon our circumstances.

In the absence of understanding the nature of happiness and how it may be found, our culture has conditioned us to believe and even expect that the constant cycle of happiness and unhappiness is normal and unavoidable. Why is this? We do not expect to cycle through periods of health and sickness on an almost daily basis, let alone numerous times within a single day. If we are sick, we consider it a signal from the body that something is wrong and needs attention.

Unhappiness is to the mind as sickness is to the body. It is a state of disharmony and imbalance. It is a signal that something is amiss and requires attention. However, in the absence of any understanding as to the real cause of unhappiness, our culture can only offer consolations and distractions.

We all feel that health is the natural state of the body. Why do we not feel that happiness is the natural state of the mind? In this book, I will suggest that it *is*, that happiness is the very nature of our being or self and, as such, lies in potential within us, accessible by all people and at all times, with the possible exception of those times when the safety and well-being of the body are compromised.

From this point of view, suffering is understood as the veiling or obscuring of our innate happiness. Thus, there is either happiness or the veiling of it, but never its absence.

All that is necessary to access our inherent happiness is to go directly into the depths of our being, behind the obscuring layers of thought and feeling. This is the great understanding that everyone should have from an early age. What could be more important in life than to know that we are already that for which we long?

This understanding is the essence of all the principal religious and spiritual traditions. However, in almost all cases it has been lost, or at least obscured, by layers of superfluous doctrines and practices that arose around the simple and direct insight upon which they were originally founded.

All the methods that are given in the various traditions have the ultimate purpose of facilitating access to the latent peace and joy that lies at the heart of all beings. The reason for so many different approaches and practices is not the complexity or inaccessibility of what is being sought. It is due partly to the differences between the cultures in which this understanding was originally formulated, and partly to the differing responses required to address people's particular difficulties and objections.

In each of these responses, this single understanding was refracted into numerous ideas and methods. However, when we distil these various approaches, they all indicate, in one way or another, that happiness is our nature, or that we are happiness itself.

THE END OF THE SEARCH

Everybody knows the experience of happiness. However, not everybody knows that happiness is the very nature of our self and can be found in the depths of our being. As a result of this overlooking of the essential nature of our self, a great search is initiated in the realm of objective experience.

In the epic poem *The Mathnawi*, Sufi poet and mystic Jelaluddin Rumi tells of a man in Cairo who dreams of a treasure buried under a certain house in Baghdad. The man sets out on an arduous journey and, after numerous trials and adventures, reaches Baghdad and finds the house that appeared to him in his dream. He knocks on the door and an elderly man answers. The traveller relates his dream and the owner of the house replies, 'That's strange, last night I dreamt of a house in Cairo under which a great treasure was buried'. The man from Cairo recognises the description of the house as his own and returns home. And sure enough, under his own home he finds a great treasure. All those years he had been sitting on it without realising it.

This is the archetypal trajectory of everyone's life: the great search for happiness in the realm of objective experience and the return to the treasure of one's own being. The out-breath and the in-breath. The adventure of becoming and the return to being. The unfolding of one's life on the horizontal dimension of time and the periodic plunge into the vertical dimension of being.

Nature provides numerous such moments: the end of seeking upon the fulfilment of a desire; a moment of astonishment; the unbearable grief at the

9

loss of a loved one; the rapture of sexual intimacy; a moment of intense danger; a glance from a friend; the silence of the forest; the peace of deep sleep. Our lives are punctuated by such moments, hairline cracks in the world which, although not discernible on the surface of experience, are portals through which we pass out of time into eternity, only to be eclipsed again by the content of experience.

The memory of such times awakens in us a nostalgia, a longing for something that is not past and forgotten but present and veiled. It lies not in the annals of the past or the promise of the future but in the depths of being.

Impelled by this longing, we embark on a great search – outwardly in the realms of objects, substances, activities and relationships, and inwardly in states of mind – frequently sampling its perfume but never finding its source. It pervades the content of experience but is never graspable *as* an experience, like a rainbow whose source can never be found. However, it cannot be found not because it is so far but because it is so close.

At the heart of all the world's great religious, spiritual and philosophical traditions lies the simple, direct means by which it may be recognised: becoming must subside in being.

Most of the time the drama of experience eclipses awareness of being. Now awareness of being outshines the drama of experience.

Awareness of being is known in each of us as the sense of 'being myself' or the knowledge 'I am' before it is coloured or qualified by experience. Therein lies the peace of our true nature. When our self is divested of all the limitations it acquires from experience, that for which we long above all else shines by itself.

In the Christian tradition, the same understanding is illustrated in the parable of the Prodigal Son. In this story, the youngest son of the king is dissatisfied with life at home and embarks on a great adventure in the world, seeking fulfilment. In spite of his numerous experiences, nothing fully satisfies him and he ends up in despair, reduced to looking after pigs and eating their food, until at last he 'comes to his senses' and remembers the abundance of his home.

This is symbolic of one who has exhausted the search for fulfilment in objective experience and recognises, or at least intuits, that they are looking for happiness in the wrong place and must return 'home'. That is, they remember the peace and happiness that is the nature of their being and re-solve to return there.

This remembrance is not the memory of something that we once possessed and have now lost, but the recognition of something that lies deep within us but that, until now, has been veiled and was thus inac-cessible.

Some of us have to go to the brink of despair before recognising that we are seeking peace and happiness in the wrong place. For others, a relatively mild dose of failure, loss or sorrow is enough to prompt the intuition that objective experience can never be a source of lasting peace and happiness, and to initi-ate an investigation into the nature of our self.

Either way, there comes a point in many of our lives when we under-stand, or at least intuit, that the peace and happiness for which we long can never be found in an object, substance, activity, circumstance or relation-ship. This understanding does not imply that we lose interest in the world or that we no longer engage with objects, activities and relationships, but simply that we no longer do so for the purpose of finding peace, happiness and love in them.

No one would be reading this book if the search for happiness in objec-tive experience had succeeded. In fact, one who is reading this book is almost certainly doing so precisely because this search has failed sufficiently often that they are at least beginning to suspect that they may be looking in the wrong place.

At some point a crisis is precipitated in our life in which we realise that we have tried everything – the conventional objects that are on offer in the world, and the less conventional states of mind that are available in the religious and spiritual traditions – and seen that nothing has ever, or could ever, give us the lasting happiness we seek.

As a result of this we may have the courage and the clarity to face a simple, unavoidable fact: nothing can make us happy! Likewise, we under-stand for the same reason that nothing can make us *unhappy*, unless and until we give it the power to, in which case it will do so.

To seek peace and happiness in objective experience is destined to fail. It is a recipe for disappointment and, in time, despair.

THE ORIGINAL PANDEMIC

At the time of writing, many people are concerned that they may be infected with a virus that will cause sickness and possibly death to themselves or their loved ones. I do not mean to disparage such concern, or the attempts that individuals, communities and nations are taking to minimise the spread of the virus. I only want to point out the attention we give to this virus whilst ignoring another malady that has infected the vast majority of people without their realising it.

This malady is the belief that peace and happiness is dependent upon external circumstances. We have allowed a single belief to steal our innate happiness, to rob us of the one thing we love above all else. And yet, so ubiquitous is this condition that we do not even realise it as such; we consider it the natural state.

This syndrome has a simple symptom: suffering! Our suffering, whether it be an intense emotion of hatred, anger or jealousy that erupts temporarily in response to a particular circumstance, or simply a mild but chronic feeling that something is missing, is the litmus test that indicates we have overlooked our essential nature or being and that, as a result, its innate peace and happiness has been obscured.

Just as physical pain is a signal from the intrinsic intelligence of the body letting us know that the body requires attention, so suffering is a message from the happiness that lies in the depths of our being: 'You are looking for me in the wrong place! I am not caused by anything outside of you. I am the nature of your being; there is no other place to find me. Turn towards me and I will take you into myself.'

As the Sufi mystic Bayazid Bastami said, 'For thirty years I sought God. But when I looked carefully I found that in reality God was the seeker and I the sought.'* Whenever we are seeking happiness, it is in fact our innate happiness that is seeking us. The happiness we seek is the happiness we are.

The great understanding that lies at the heart of all the main religious and spiritual traditions consists of two essential insights: happiness is the very nature of our self, and we share our being with everyone and everything.

---

*As quoted in James Fadiman and Robert Frager, *Essential Sufism* (HarperCollins, 1997).

The second insight will be touched upon towards the end of this book. As regards the first, in order to liberate this happiness from its hiding place in the depths of our being and bring it out into our lived and felt experience, it is necessary to go to one's essential being or self and recognise its nature.

This is why self-knowledge stands as the foundation of all the major religious and spiritual traditions. It is the great understanding that gives us access to the peace and happiness that is our very nature.

CHAPTER TWO

Know Thyself

*Every living being longs always to be happy, untainted
by sorrow; and everyone has the greatest love for their self,
which is solely due to the fact that happiness is their real
nature. Hence, in order to realise that inherent and
untainted happiness, which indeed one daily experiences
when the mind is subdued in deep sleep, it is essential
that one should know oneself.*

RAMANA MAHARSHI

In the Christian tradition it is said, 'The kingdom of heaven is within you'.
What is the kingdom of heaven if not a realm of eternal happiness? The essential message of Christianity is that this realm of eternal happiness lies
within us; it is the nature of our being.

In the Vedantic tradition of India we find the same understanding condensed into three Sanskrit words, *sat chit ananda*. *Sat* refers to being, *chit* to
knowing, consciousness or awareness, and *ananda* to peace or happiness.
Thus, *sat chit ananda* means simply that to know the nature of one's being
is happiness itself.

In Buddhism it is said that the very nature of one's mind is inherently free
from any imperfection. Cautious not to objectify happiness as a state of mind,
the Buddhist teaching refers to it simply as the end of suffering. Thus, all that
is required to access that happiness is to know the nature of one's mind.

Indeed, if we were to distil the essential understanding contained in all
the great religious, spiritual and philosophical traditions into a single phrase,
it would read something like this: 'Happiness is your nature' or 'You are happiness itself'.

It follows that in order to access the peace and happiness for which all
people long above all else, all that is necessary is to understand the nature of
one's self. For this reason, the words *Know Thyself* were carved onto the

entrance to the temple of Apollo in Delphi, thus standing at the very origin of Western civilisation.

We all seek happiness, but most of us seek it in *objective experience*. In the approach that is being suggested in this book, we seek peace and happiness *at its source*, namely, in our self or our being. For this reason it is sometimes referred to as the direct path to peace and happiness.

A SOFTENING OF ATTENTION

What does it mean to know oneself? In the early 1980s, I went with my brother Andrew to a series of Alfred Brendel's recitals of Beethoven's piano sonatas in London. During these recitals my attention was in general fully absorbed in the music, but from time to time I noticed a softening of its focus.

On one occasion, my attention relaxed sufficiently that I became aware not only of the music but of the fact that I was listening to the music. In other words, *I became aware that I was aware.*

There was nothing extraordinary about this. On the contrary, the fact of simply being aware, or awareness itself, was clearly the most familiar and intimate aspect of my experience. However, I had previously overlooked it, so exclusively focused was I on my experience – on this occasion, the content of the music.

In time, my attention was again drawn to the music, but I noticed that at certain points during the recital it spontaneously disengaged from it and returned effortlessly to the fact of being aware. It even felt at times as if my attention were being pulled backwards, away from its content, towards the fact of simply being aware, or awareness itself.

After some time, I noticed that I had the ability to travel backwards and forwards with my attention, between the music in the foreground and the presence of awareness in the background.

I began to explore this new faculty, and at some point it became clear that in between the background of being aware and the foreground of the music there was an intermediary layer of experience, a middle ground, so to speak, of thoughts, feelings and sensations of the body.

There were now three elements of my experience: one, the external world (consisting of the concert hall, the audience and the music); two, my mind and body (comprising the internal world of thoughts, feelings and sensations); and three, in the background, the fact of being aware or awareness itself.

It was as if I had taken a step back from my mind and body, with which I normally identified myself. They were now part of the foreground of my experience and I was standing as the presence of awareness behind them, watching them just as I was watching the performance.

As my attention travelled back and forth between these three realms, it occurred to me that the person I normally considered myself to be – my mind and body – was itself part of the objective content of experience that I was aware *of*, along with the auditorium, the audience and the music.

In particular, I noticed that my thoughts and feelings were a layer of experience that not only was added to my experience of the world, like subtitles superimposed upon a movie, but also through which I interpreted the world.

Some time later I would also notice that my experience of the world was itself filtered through my sense perceptions, which impose their own limitations on whatever is perceived. This would, in turn, give rise to the question as to what the world is in itself, beyond these limitations. But for now, this challenge to my customary sense of myself was enough.

A SHIFT IN IDENTITY

At some point a question spontaneously arose in my mind: Who am I really? Am I the thoughts, feelings and sensations that I am aware of, or am I the one that is aware of them?

I was familiar with the Indian sage Ramana Maharshi's use of such questions, a method known as 'self-enquiry', but had found it rather heady and abstract. No doubt the question that emerged at this stage was prompted by my previous interest in these matters, but nevertheless it arose in me this time as if for the first time and was profoundly connected to my experience.

This questioning was not just a mental exercise. Nor was it a method I was practising in order to bring about a certain result. It seemed to be taking place spontaneously, although I was cooperating with it.

It became obvious that whatever it is that knows our thoughts and images is not *itself* a thought or image. What is that?

Whatever it is that is aware of our feelings and sensations is not *itself* a feeling or sensation. What is that?

Whatever it is that perceives the world is not *itself* a sight, sound, taste, texture or smell. What is that?

It is simply that which knows or is aware. It is our self. It is awareness or consciousness itself.*

Until this recognition I had considered myself to be a person, a body-mind, an amalgam of thoughts, feelings and sensations. It seemed to be myself *as this person* who was aware of the world. As such, I considered awareness an *attribute* of the body-mind, a faculty that I as a person *possessed*.

I now realised that the person I previously imagined myself to be was something that I was *aware of*, along with my experience of the world.

I recognised that I was essentially *that which knows* or *is aware of* the entire content of experience, including the thoughts, images, memories, feelings and sensations that constitute the mind and body.

I realised that it is not myself as a *person* who is aware of the world, but rather myself as *awareness* that is aware of the person and the world.

The transition from the belief that we are a person with the faculty of awareness to the understanding that we are awareness itself may seem like a small step, but it has enormous implications for any individual and for the evolution of humanity as a whole. Indeed, I would suggest that it is the next evolutionary step, and that upon which the survival of humanity, as we know it, depends.

The understanding 'I am awareness' is the first great understanding.

This is not an extraordinary recognition or something that is difficult to access. In fact, it is enshrined in common parlance. We say, '*I know* my thoughts and images', '*I am aware of* feelings and sensations' and '*I perceive* the world'.

In each of these statements, we recognise ourself as the *knowing, aware* or *perceiving* element, and thoughts, images, feelings, sensations and perceptions as *objects* that we know, are aware of or perceive.

In other words, we are not essentially our thoughts, images, memories or stories about our life; *we are that which knows them*. We are not essentially our feelings or sensations; *we are that which is aware of them*. We are not the

---

*The terms 'awareness' and 'consciousness' are used synonymously throughout this book.

sights, sounds, tastes, textures and smells that constitute our experience of the world; *we are that which perceives them.*

We are nothing that is experienced; *we are that which experiences.*

We are not essentially anything that we are aware *of*; we are simply the fact of knowing, being aware or awareness itself.

LETTING GO

I understand that I'm not my body or mind, but who would I be if I were to let go of everyone and everything with which I associate and identify myself?

You would be the same inherently peaceful and unconditionally fulfilled self that you are now, although you do not currently recognise your self as such because of your entanglement in, or identification with, the content of experience. The only difference is that what you now consider a distant possibility would become your lived and felt experience.

Every night you willingly and effortlessly let go of everyone and everything with whom you associate or identify and fall deeply asleep. In the experience of deep sleep you are all alone. Everything that is not essential to you has been removed and, as a result, you experience the peace of your true nature.

If letting go of everyone and everything were a traumatic or frightening experience, we would dread falling asleep at night. But we look forward to it! Why? Because it gives us access to the peace of our true nature, which is veiled by the activities of thinking, feeling, acting and relating during the day.

In fact, when we fall asleep we do not enter a new state. We are always essentially the presence of awareness. However, during the waking and dreaming states, we forget or overlook this or, more accurately, it is obscured by thoughts, feelings, sensations and perceptions. In these two states awareness is so thoroughly mixed with the content of experience that it is not recognised as such. It is veiled by experience.

Likewise, when we emerge from deep sleep into the dreaming and waking states, the presence of the awareness that we essentially are does not change or disappear. It is simply veiled by experience. Our essential self of pure awareness does not need to be liberated. It is already and inherently free of the content of experience.

So it is not necessary to let go of anyone or anything. All that is required is to recognise our essential nature of pure awareness that lies behind all experience and shines in the midst of all experience.

Nor will you lose your ability to think, feel, act, perceive and relate. On the contrary, these activities will be greatly enhanced by this new understanding of your self, for the one on whose behalf they arise, and in whose service they are undertaken, will be clearly known.

CHAPTER THREE

Are You My Self?

*Home is neither here nor there. Home is within you,
or home is nowhere at all.*

HERMAN HESSE

*If the presence of awareness is the primary fact of experience, why are most of us
not in touch with it?*

It is simply because we become lost in or identified with the content of our
experience. If someone were to ask us to look around the room in which we
are currently sitting and describe what we are experiencing, most of us would
refer to chairs, books, papers, photographs, paintings, a table, and so on.

Very few would mention the space of the room. Why not? We overlook
the space because it has no objective features that can be seen, heard, tasted,
touched or smelt. At the same time, we cannot say that we are not experiencing it.

Likewise, if someone were to ask us to describe our current experience
in general, almost all of us would list our thoughts, images, memories, feelings, sensations of the body, perceptions of the world, activities, relationships,
and so on. Very few of us would mention the presence of awareness. Why
not?

The fact of being aware is the most obvious, intimate and familiar element
of experience, and yet it has no objective features. Like space, it cannot be
seen, heard, tasted, touched or smelt. It is, so to speak, transparent; it is silent
and empty. And yet without it there can be no experience.

THE OVERLOOKING OF OUR TRUE NATURE

It is inconceivable that a landscape painter would spend her life painting in
nature, noticing the trees, fields, animals, flowers and clouds, without ever

noticing sunlight. The light cannot be seen directly, and yet it is that which renders the world visible. Indeed, it is all she truly sees!

Likewise, awareness renders all experience knowable. It is for this reason that awareness is said to be luminous. It is the illuminating or knowing factor in all experience. It is, as such, the primary and most important element of experience, and yet it is almost always overlooked or ignored in favour of the objective content of experience.

Consider the amount of knowledge and experience that each of us acquired during our education. Did any of our parents or teachers ever ask us what it is that knows or is aware of that knowledge and experience? I have yet to meet anyone who answers 'yes' to that question.

Is it not extraordinary that, as a culture, we have almost universally overlooked the primary and most important element of experience? And could there be anything more interesting than to know the nature of that through which everything else is known? Indeed, would it be possible to know what anything truly is without first knowing the nature of that with which it is known?

The fact of knowing, being aware or awareness itself is closer to us than our breathing, our innermost thoughts or our most cherished feelings. In fact, it is not *close* to us; it *is* what we essentially are. It is overlooked precisely because it is so intimate and familiar, not because it is remote, unknown or inaccessible.

It is sometimes said that awareness transcends experience, implying that it lies *beyond* experience and is, as such, out of reach, unknowable and mysterious. Nothing could be further from the truth. Awareness lies *behind* the layer of thinking, feeling and sensing with which we normally identify ourself and is *prior* to it, just as a screen could be said to lie behind and be prior to the movie that appears on it.

Awareness is not overlooked because it is unknown but because it is so *well known*. Familiarity, in this case, may not breed contempt, but it certainly accounts for neglect. We tend to overlook the space of a room or the light in a landscape because our attention is exclusively focused on objects. However, as soon as our attention relaxes, we become aware of the space or the light.

Similarly, we overlook the presence of awareness due to the exclusive focus of our attention on the content of experience, that is, our thoughts, feelings, sensations, perceptions, activities and relationships. However, awareness is like the space or the light: as soon as our attention relaxes, we become aware of it.

It is for this reason that in the Tantric tradition of Kashmir Shaivism it is said that awareness is 'the greatest secret, more hidden than the most concealed and yet more evident than the most evident of things'.*

When I suggest that we overlook the presence of awareness in the same way that we overlook the space in a room or sunlight in the landscape, I imply that we are one thing and awareness another. This is not intended. *We are awareness!*

It is we, awareness, who, directing the light of our attention towards the objective content of experience, overlook our self, the subject of experience. When the focus of our attention softens and we become aware that we are aware, it is we, awareness, who relax our attention from its objective content and, as a result, become aware of our self.

We come back to our self; we remember our self. However, this is not a remembrance of something that was once known and subsequently forgotten. It is the recognition of what we always and already are but usually overlook or ignore.

We might call this overlooking or forgetting of the presence of awareness the original ADD – Awareness Deficit Disorder – from which the vast majority of humans suffer unknowingly. It is the cause of all psychological suffering of the individual, and the conflicts between individuals, communities and nations.

In the Vedantic tradition it is referred to as ignorance, in the sense of ignoring our true nature, and in Christianity as Original Sin, that is, the initial error from which all subsequent errors are compounded.

The fact of knowing, being aware or awareness itself is not something that some people have in greater measure than others, nor is it more readily accessible to some people than to others. None has privileged access to it. It is available to all people, at all times and under all circumstances, simply by virtue of the fact that everybody is aware, irrespective of what they may be aware of in any moment of experience.

*Thanks to Mark S. G. Dyczkowski for this quotation.

It can be easily recognised as soon as we soften the focus of our attention from its objective content and come back to our self. It is the silent presence behind and within all experience.

RETURNING TO THE PRESENCE OF AWARENESS

After the experience at the concert in London, I noticed often over the next few weeks that there were gaps in the flow of experience during which my attention would be gently drawn back to the fact of being aware. It was as though attention were a two-way street that could be travelled in one direction, towards the content of experience, and in the opposite direction, towards myself, the presence of awareness.

I also noticed that the intermediary layer of thoughts and feelings was frequently provoked in response to my experience of the world. If I liked whatever I was experiencing, I would seek to hold on to it; if I disliked it, I would attempt to get rid of it.

In other words, I noticed that experience was often accompanied by a sense of dissatisfaction. Sometimes this dissatisfaction was barely discernible, such as a feeling of boredom or a sense of lack that was not intense enough to command my attention but kept me, without my realising it, in a more or less continuous state of seeking and resisting.

On other occasions the dissatisfaction was fully felt in the form of suffering. Whenever I noticed this, I would make a conscious effort to return to the presence of awareness in the background of experience, for I had already noticed that, being devoid of all objective qualities, it was the place of peace or refuge in myself.

Sometimes this was easy and required almost no effort, and at other times there was some reluctance. It was in response to this reluctance that I began to develop a regular habit or practice of returning my attention to its source in the presence of awareness.

This new habit was very simple. As a child I was brought up with P. D. Eastman's book *Are You My Mother?*, in which a recently hatched baby bird is separated from its mother and sets off in search of her. After some time, the bird encounters a kitten and asks it, 'Are you my mother?' 'No', replies the kitten. Next it comes across a hen. 'Are you my mother?' it asks. 'No', replies the hen.

The baby bird continues on its journey asking everything that it encounters – a dog, a cow, a car, a boat and an aeroplane – the same question. Finally, the bird is returned to its nest and reunited with its mother.

The practice of stepping back from the content of experience and resting in and as the presence of awareness proceeds in a similar way. We simply ask every experience that we encounter, 'Are you myself?'

When we see a mountain, a building, a person or a movie, we do not mistake it for ourself. They are what we *know* or *experience*, not what we *are*.

Likewise, when we encounter a thought, image, feeling or sensation, we simply enquire, 'Are you what I essentially am?' These are objects of experience that are known, witnessed or experienced by us, that is, by awareness. We are no more our thoughts, images, feelings and sensations than we are a mountain, a tree or a movie.

This simple question invites a softening of the focus of our attention from its objective content and facilitates the recognition of our self as the witnessing or knowing presence of awareness.

Most people are so accustomed to paying exclusive attention to the content of their experience that this process of stepping back and resting as the presence of awareness may seem, to begin with, to involve some effort or practice.

In this case, we may ask ourself a question such as, 'Who am I really?', 'What is it that knows or is aware of my experience?', 'What is the continuous element in all changing experience?' or 'What is it that cannot be removed or separated from me?'

Each of these is a variation of the same question, what I call the 'sacred question', whose purpose is to gently invite our attention away from its objective content and back to our self, the presence of awareness. That is the essence of self-enquiry.

As an alternative to this line of questioning, we may also reason that nothing that appears and disappears in our experience could be essential to us. Only the fact of being aware remains consistently present, and therefore only the fact of being aware qualifies as our essential self.

For a while, the pull of objective experience may be so strong that it only seems possible to remain knowingly the presence of awareness for brief periods, and questions or lines of reasoning such as these may need to be repeated. However, every time we return to awareness, we are eroding the old habit of losing ourself in the content of experience and, although we may not realise it to begin with, establishing ourself in our true nature.

In time, it becomes so natural to understand and feel ourself as the presence of awareness that it no longer needs to be maintained by effort or practice, nor does it need to be initiated by a question or a line of reasoning.

Just as previously we did not need to remind ourself continually that we were a man or a woman, because it was simply our default identity, so now it is no longer necessary to remind ourself, or make the effort, to be knowingly the presence of awareness. It simply becomes our new identity. There may still be moments of forgetting, but these occur less frequently and endure for less time.

Somebody once asked the Indian sage Atmananda Krishna Menon how one knows when one is established in one's true nature and he replied, 'When thoughts, feelings, sensations and perceptions can no longer take you away from your self'.

As the content of our experience gradually loses its capacity to take us away from our self, it is no longer necessary to turn away from it. We remain knowingly the presence of awareness both in formal periods of meditation, when we withdraw our attention from the content of experience, and during everyday life, in the midst of experience.

The dilemma of attention is resolved. The conflict between awareness and experience diminishes. Experience becomes increasingly transparent to the presence of awareness and we find ourself at home everywhere.

CHAPTER FOUR

The Art of Self-Enquiry

Of all the koans, 'I' is the most profound.

IKKYU

Can you give an example of self-enquiry in action?

I remember a young man who attended one of my retreats several years ago. His face bore the marks of a lifetime of suffering. During the retreat I could feel his resistance wanting to formulate itself as a question, and a few days before the end he challenged my suggestion that his nature is inherently peaceful: 'If my essential nature is freedom, peace and happiness, why do I suffer so much of the time?'

I suggested that it was simply because he had lost himself in, or identified himself with, the content of his experience. 'But my experience is so intense and overwhelming much of the time', he replied, 'that I don't know how to *disidentify* myself from it'.

'It would only be necessary to disidentify yourself from the content of experience', I suggested, 'if you were identical to it in the first place.

'Does the space in a room have to work hard not to identify itself with the four walls of the room, or to let go of all the objects or people as they leave the room? It would only have to do so if it were attached to them in the first place. The space of the room is already and inherently free and at rest.

'You are like that', I suggested. 'You only need recognise yourself as such.'

'So what's keeping me from doing that?' he asked.

'Just an old, conditioned habit', I replied. 'Our culture has educated us to believe certain things about ourselves from an early age and we do so without question. This may work, more or less, for a while, but sooner or later the suffering that inevitably attends these assumptions compels us to question them. The primary assumption is that our essential self or being is conditioned by, and limited to, the content of experience.'

After giving the young man a moment to take this in, I asked him to tell us about his self.

'When I first arrived at this retreat…' he began.

I stopped him. 'You are describing a memory. We want to know about your *self*.'

'I feel like I'm destined to suffer all my life', he said, with an air of resignation.

'Now you are telling us about a feeling, not about your self. Your feelings appear to you, they arise within you, they may linger for some time and they may be familiar and repetitive, but sooner or later they vanish. When you say "I feel", tell us about the one you refer to as "I", not about *what* you feel.'

'I think it's –'

'Don't tell us about your thoughts!' I interrupted, to keep him from taking another step in the wrong direction. 'Tell us about the "I" to whom your thoughts appear.'

'I…' There was a long silence.

'Perfect!' I said quietly. Although reluctant to disturb the silence, I did so because I sensed thought beginning to take over again. 'You have the undeniable sense of simply being. "I" is the name you give to that being. Tell us more.'

'I am…' Another long silence followed. By this stage the man's eyes were closed and I could see that the tension on his face had already diminished.

I could tell how sincerely and intently he was participating in our conversation. He was giving his attention exclusively to his self, to the fact of simply being, before it was qualified in any way by his experience. There was no struggle with the content of experience; he had simply become more interested in the nature of his self.

It was clear that it was no longer necessary to guide him through a series of questions, nor even to interpret his experience. One could have heard a pin drop in the room of two hundred people. I could feel that we were all sharing the same experience, participating in the experience of simply being.

He opened his eyes and, with a broad smile, asked, 'Is it that simple?' But his rhetorical question required no response. His experience was its own evidence.

TRACING OUR WAY BACK TO OUR SELF

Later in the day the man asked, 'But what if all the old suffering comes back?'

'It probably will', I admitted, 'through force of habit. A glimpse of our true nature doesn't erase years of conditioning. In almost all cases, the old conditioning will return.

'But whenever it does, all that is necessary is to trace your way back to your essential being as you just have, and rest there, as that. Every time you do so you are weakening the old habit of becoming lost in or identified with the content of your experience, and instead are becoming established in your true nature of peace.'

We didn't speak again for a day or so, but I noticed that whereas previously he had kept himself apart from the group, he was now talking enthusiastically with other attendees and participating in shared activities, such as meals and afternoon walks in the countryside. On the last day he was eager to ask another question.

'I understood when you suggested all I had to do was trace my way back to my true nature and rest there. So I kept doing that, but after a while I noticed that I couldn't find that self who was tracing its way back to my true nature. There's just me, that peaceful presence. Does that make sense?'

'It does make sense', I replied, and explained to him that the suggestion to trace one's way back to one's true nature and rest there, as that, is a compassionate concession that is given to one who believes and feels that they are a suffering self.

'If I had suggested to you a couple of days ago', I said, 'that the self on whose behalf your suffering arises is an illusion and, therefore, by implication, that your suffering itself is an illusion, I suspect that you would have been frustrated. Another layer of resistance would have been added to your current experience of suffering, simply compounding it.

'So I gave the apparently suffering self something to do: trace your way back to your self, and remain resting in your being at all times. Having tried this only a few times, you brought yourself to the understanding that you are always and already the inherently peaceful and unconditionally fulfilled presence of awareness. It is not something you become through effort or practice. You simply recognise it is what you always and already are. That is, it recognises itself, in you, as you.'

'Is there something else I should do now?' he asked.

'If this is clear', I suggested, 'nothing remains to be done. Who would do it, and to what end? The question of doing something or not doing something simply no longer arises. However, if it is not clear, that is, if suffering arises again, see that it arises on behalf of the temporary, finite self that, at least in that moment, you believe yourself to be.

'Once again you can simply trace your way back to your inherently peaceful and unconditionally fulfilled nature of pure awareness. In time, the appearance of suffering, the recognition of the false assumption on whose behalf it arises and the return to your being will be almost simultaneous. You begin to be established in your true nature.

'As soon as the suffering arises, it is met with the mirror of understanding and effortlessly dissolves. Self-enquiry gives way to self-abidance. The happiness we seek is revealed as the happiness we are.'

This understanding is the fulfilment of the search. It brings us back to the place from which we never really departed. We left home and set out on a great adventure seeking peace and fulfilment, only to find ourself back at home again, as if for the first time.

In fact, we didn't even leave home. It is more like one who falls asleep and dreams that they embark on an epic journey. They pass through many traumatic childhood experiences, grow up, get married, have a family, struggle to earn a living, grow old, become sick and die. And as they die, they wake up to find that they were lying peacefully on their bed all along.

The journey is the pathless path from our self to our self, from the happiness we seek to the happiness we are. Ironically, it is almost always necessary to embark on some sort of journey before this becomes clear. It is for this reason that Bayazid Bastami said, 'That for which we long cannot be found by seeking, and yet only seekers find it'.*

*   *   *

*As quoted in James Fadiman and Robert Frager, *Essential Sufism* (HarperCollins, 1997).

I'm haunted by the feeling of being a failure and not having fulfilled my poten-
tial in life. I've tried so many approaches to help with this but it just persists.
Can the practice of self-enquiry help me?

In this approach we don't pay much attention to the feeling of failure or lack
of fulfilment. Instead we go directly to the core of the issue, the 'I' on whose
behalf such feelings arise.

All our emotional or psychological suffering arises on behalf of that one,
so by resolving this issue once and for all, we do not simply take care of the
feeling of being a failure or unfulfilled; we take care of the *source* of all afflictive emotions.

When we explore the 'I' around whom our suffering revolves, we don't
find a self who is frustrated, unfulfilled, anxious, lonely, ashamed, and so on.
We find our essential being, which is completely free of any such feelings.
That is to say, it finds or recognises itself. It is open, empty, at peace and
without any sense of lack. This is our natural state.

In fact, it is not even necessary to conceptualise it as peace and happiness.
We do so only in order to contrast it with our previous state of disturbance
and lack. Once we have been accustomed to this natural condition for some
time, it simply becomes our new norm.

All that is necessary is to remain in touch with our self, the inherently
peaceful and unconditionally fulfilled presence of awareness, until this becomes our new, felt sense of self. In fact, it is not really a *new* sense of self.
It is simply the familiar sense of self that always accompanies us, that *is* us,
but is now relieved of its previous agitation and sense of lack.

The feeling of dissatisfaction which has accompanied us for most of our
life simply leaves us, not because we have done anything to it but because
we have undermined the assumption upon which it arose. We feel fulfilled,
but for no particular reason.

All our physical and mental faculties remain intact. They are simply relieved of the tyranny of the separate self and, as a result, are now free to be
used in service of the qualities that are inherent in us, namely peace, joy, love
and freedom.

* * *

How can one evaluate the authenticity of a teaching?

One of the hallmarks of a true teaching is that it is not affiliated with any particular position, attitude or practice. It is not a body of knowledge and practices that is disseminated like a maths or history curriculum. It is simply a spontaneous response to a situation or question that comes directly from understanding or love.

Understanding and love do not have a form of their own and are, therefore, free to assume any shape or action that is perfectly tailored to a particular circumstance or question, just as a bucket dipped into the ocean will draw out a measure of water that is uniquely and exquisitely fitted to its own proportions.

A true teaching cannot be evaluated by its form or content alone but by the source from which it originates. Any expression that originates in understanding or love contains within it a particular quality, a power even, that has the ability to take the recipient to the same source of understanding and love in their self. The teaching is simply the means by which they are given experiential access to this understanding and love.

The finite mind superimposes its own limitations on everything that it knows or perceives and, therefore, cannot find happiness or know the ultimate reality. For this reason, the teaching will often refuse to entertain the mind on its own terms and will find ways of exposing and undermining it. As a result, such a teaching may give one person a practice and in the next moment, in response to another question, refuse to suggest any such practice.

For some people, just a few words of guidance will be sufficient. However, if a person has an inquisitive and sophisticated mind, then it is likely that they will raise objections and question every aspect of the teaching. If such a mind is not acknowledged and honoured, it tends to become frustrated and angry.

In order to pave the way for the understanding and love that is the essence of the teaching to be taken deeply into the heart and body, it will, in such cases, be necessary to elaborate refined lines of reasoning. For such people, it is only when the mind's objections and questions have been met satisfactorily that they will be open to a new possibility.

In this case, the teaching will give the mind complete freedom to explore these matters as much as it wishes, and even encourage it to do so, thereby allowing it gradually, naturally and effortlessly to bring itself to its own end.

CHAPTER FIVE

The Essence of Meditation

*There is a huge silence inside each of us
that beckons us into itself.*

MEISTER ECKHART

The recognition of our true nature is not a new experience that happens to us. It is the revealing or the noticing of what we always and already are but often overlook due to our exclusive fascination with the content of experience.

It is we, awareness, who, being intimately one with all experience, seem to lose our self in it, thereby overlooking our innate peace and happiness. The inevitable suffering that ensues from this is a call from our self to our self – a call to return home from the adventure of experience in which we have become entangled.

In this recognition we do not cease being one kind of self and become another kind of self. We simply cease losing our self in or identifying our self with the content of experience, and we recognise our self as the inherently peaceful presence of awareness that lies behind it.

We cannot *become* what we always and already are, and we cannot *be* what we are not. We can only cease imagining and feeling that we are something other than the presence of awareness. Once we have disentangled our self from the content of experience, our true nature simply shines by itself, just as the blue sky is revealed when the clouds disperse.

DISENTANGLING OUR SELF

If the forgetting or ignoring of our essential self is the veiling of our innate happiness and the ultimate cause of psychological suffering, then the remembrance or clear knowledge of our essential self is the means by which this forgetfulness or ignorance is *removed* and our innate peace and happiness revealed.

If someone believes they have COVID-19, they may take a test. If the test comes back negative, their ignorance of their state of health is simply removed. The removal of ignorance cannot be said to be the *cause* of their good health. It simply allows what is already the case to be fully acknowledged. Likewise, the recognition of our true nature is not the *cause* of happiness; it is simply the removal of the ignorance of our true nature. It is the uncovering of our being, whose nature is happiness itself.

Meditation is the relaxing of the focus of our attention from its content, the disentangling of our self from the drama of experience, and the subsequent emergence of our essential nature of silent awareness.

It is simply the process whereby our essential nature or being is revealed, after it is divested of all the qualities or characteristics that it acquires from experience. Instead of allowing our attention to become mixed with the content of experience, we trace it back in the opposite direction. In the absence of anything to hold on to, attention can no longer stand and is dissolved in its source of pure awareness.

This recognition of the essential nature of our self is traditionally referred to as enlightenment, awakening, salvation or satori. However, enlightenment is not an extraordinary, mystical or exotic experience. In fact, it is not an objective experience at all. Somebody once asked the Zen teacher Shunryu Suzuki why he never spoke of his enlightenment experience, and his wife, who was sitting at the back of the hall, stood up and said, 'Because he never had one!' Our essential being or true nature of pure awareness simply ceases to be veiled or 'endarkened' by experience and, as a result, stands revealed.

DIRECT AND INDIRECT PATHS

This return to our being, which is referred to in many different ways in the religious and spiritual traditions, constitutes the essence of meditation. It is sometimes referred to as the Direct Path, as it is the means by which we go directly to the happiness that is the nature of our being, rather than via an object such as a mantra, the breath or a teacher.

Ramana Maharshi referred to it as 'sinking the mind into the heart'. Jesus referred to it as 'entering into thy closet, closing thy door and praying to thy Father, who is in secret', that is, returning one's attention to one's being and resting there quietly, all alone.

This return to our being and its inherent peace is often initiated by an investigation, and hence its name, self-enquiry. However, once the enquiry has brought about the letting go of everything with which we normally identify our self, no further investigation is required. Self-enquiry gives way to self-abiding, self-remembering or simply resting in being, as being.

It is in this self-resting that the unlimited and inherently peaceful nature of our being reveals itself, either gradually or suddenly. The memory of our eternity emerges, not from the past but from the depths of our being, where it is lying quietly all the time.

Thus, the essence of meditation is simply to be aware of being. And as we are always aware of simply being, meditation ultimately is not something we do. It is what we are.

In the context of this understanding, what is the purpose of meditations that involve focusing our attention on something like a mantra, an image, a flame, the breath or the pause between breaths?

Many of us are so accustomed to giving our attention exclusively to the content of experience that bringing our attention back to rest in the heart of awareness may, initially, be too much of a confrontation. The gravitational pull of thoughts and feelings, the experience of the body and world, and the demand of activities and relationships is simply too strong.

So, as a compassionate concession to such a mind, the religious and spiritual traditions suggest a compromise whereby they give the mind an object on which to focus, by way of preparation for its ultimate subsidence in the heart of awareness. Such an object is a half-way stage between the finite mind and its essence.

In this case, the mind which is usually dispersed amongst the objects of experience is brought to settle on a single object. Not only does this bring the disparate energies of the mind to rest, but it also infuses the mind with the particular quality of the object itself.

For instance, a mantra, although it may be only a single syllable, is the distilled essence of centuries of understanding and is considered, as such, to contain this understanding encoded within it. Not only does the repetition of such a sound bring the mind to rest on a single object, but the pre-verbal understanding that lies within it, in the form of a subtle vibration, gradually permeates the mind, infusing it with its innate intelligence.

The same principle lies behind the power of music. Rock music has the capacity to arouse and articulate instinctive impulses in the body. Folk music can awaken the deepest longing in our hearts. And in listening to Bach or Beethoven, one may intuit that the very structure of the universe is being revealed in a way that can never be grasped by the narrow compass of the mind.

It is no coincidence that in classical Greek thought, the Logos or Word is considered the first form of divine love and intelligence, through which it manifests as the universe. Conversely, music in general, and a mantra in particular, are means by which we may return to this love and intelligence.

The object could also be the breath. It is significant that in Latin both the word *spiritus,* from which our word 'spirit' is derived, and the word *anima*, which refers to the soul or individual, can be translated as 'breath' or 'breathing'. Thus, the breath was seen as the principle in a living being which connects it to its divine or universal origin.

Focusing attention on the breath is considered a powerful practice because it not only steadies the mind but also infuses it with its transparency, thereby preparing it for its final dissolution in the emptiness of awareness.

Some traditions recommend that in meditation we give attention to an image of our teacher, and that in life in general we devote ourself to the person of the teacher. Entering into such a devotional relationship obviously has many potential pitfalls, but let us briefly consider the understanding that lies behind it.

If correctly understood, the teacher is not a person as such but rather the impersonal functioning of love and intelligence. In giving one's attention to a teacher, such as the Buddha, Jesus or Ramana Maharshi, one is placing one's own mind in their mind, thereby clothing the individual mind in the divine mind, until, through continual acquaintance, it becomes subsumed by it. In the Sufi tradition it is referred to as 'clothing oneself in the teacher'.

I first met Francis Lucille in 1996 and immediately recognised that he would be the person to guide me to the recognition of my true nature. That is, he became my teacher and, later on, a close friend. For many years we used to host retreats for him in our home in Shropshire, and at the end of one such retreat I found that he had left one of his tee shirts in my bedroom drawer. I immediately recognised it as a symbol of the unique quality of friendship that develops between a teacher and student, which often requires no verbal or formal acknowledgement.

These examples are just some of the ways the religious and spiritual traditions have used the object-facing tendency of the mind as a means whereby the mind itself may be divested of its objective content and its essence of pure awareness revealed.

Many of us also enact these sacred rituals in our homes without necessarily realising it. A vase of flowers on the mantelpiece, a bowl on the table, a carefully prepared meal, a painting on the wall: all such objects are invitations to the mind to return from its adventure in the past and future to the sanctity of the now, in which we stand at one with our experience, divested of the subject–object relationship.

If we are to find the peace and happiness for which we long above all else, we must, in one way or another, directly or indirectly, disentangle our self from the content of experience and recognise our essential, uncoloured, unqualified being.

Until recently, the Direct Path that is being suggested here was not widely available, or if it was, it was couched in language that made it seem complex and unattainable. For this reason alone, many of us started on an indirect path.

During the first conversation I ever had with Francis, he asked me how I had come by my great love of truth. I explained that my mother had introduced me to the non-dual tradition in my teens, and went on to describe the various pathways and practices I had explored over the following twenty years. Because these practices had either been devotional in nature or required the directing of attention towards an object, a mantra in my case, I lamented the fact that it had taken me so long to find this simple, direct approach.

Francis immediately replied that they were not wasted years. They were exactly what I had needed by way of preparation, he said, and had enabled me to understand the truth that I had heard from him at our first meeting. After a long silence, he added, 'How beautiful, the mother handing her son back to God'.

THE FOCUSING AND RELAXING OF ATTENTION

There seem to be so many different types of meditation. How do we decide which one is best for us?

All meditation practice can be divided into two categories, each defined by its use of attention. In the indirect approach described above, attention is focused; in the direct approach, it is relaxed. In order to distinguish between them, it is helpful to understand what is meant by 'attention'.

The word 'attention' comes from two Latin words, *ad*, meaning 'to' or 'towards', and *tendere*, meaning 'to stretch', implying that attention is a 'stretching' or directing of awareness towards an object of experience.

When we say 'I know a thought' or 'I perceive the tree', the word 'I' refers to our self, awareness, the subject of experience that knows or is aware, and 'a thought' or 'the tree' refers to the object that is known or perceived. Knowing and perceiving are the pathways of attention that connect the subject to the object.

The directing of awareness towards an object of experience could be likened to the stretching of a rubber band. In order to stretch a rubber band, both of its ends must be secured. This sets up a tension within it. Directing one's attention towards an object in meditation is like stretching a rubber band between two points, between the subject that knows and the object that is known. It requires an effort. Whilst this effort may initially be necessary to gather and steady the mind, ultimately it creates a state of tension that cannot bring about peace.

If attention could be considered the 'stretching' of awareness towards an object, then the ultimate meditation is the relaxation of that movement. The effort of attention must be relaxed. Once the mind has become accustomed to resting steadily on its selected object, we let go of the object and allow attention to flow back to its source of pure awareness. Just as a rubber band spontaneously reverts to its relaxed condition when one of its ends is released, so our attention naturally sinks back into the awareness from which it arises when its object is released. Attention is relieved of its tension.

In this way, the mind, divested of its dynamism, is revealed as pure awareness. That is the experience of peace. So do not worry about what sort of meditation to practise; sooner or later all rivers lose their dynamism and return to the ocean.

Why do we lose ourselves so easily and frequently in experience?

It is we, awareness, who being utterly, intimately one with experience, become lost in it. As the visionary poet and artist William Blake said, 'Eternity is in love with the productions of time'.*

However, awareness pays for this love with its own innate happiness, just as a mother at times forgoes her own happiness for the sake of her child. At some point, the ensuing suffering compels awareness to extricate itself from the content of experience and return to itself. And it returns home on the same path by which it left: the path of attention.

Previously we, awareness, directed our attention towards, and seemed to lose ourself in, the content of experience. Now we retrace our steps in the opposite direction, backwards, inwards or self-wards, withdrawing our attention from its content, thereby extricating ourself from the drama of experience and returning to our being, where our innate happiness is found quietly shining.

*　　*　　*

Is there such a thing as meditating too much?

It depends on what you mean by meditation. If you mean focusing your attention on an object, then yes, there is such a thing as too much meditation. If you consider by the word 'meditation' resting in and as the presence of awareness, then there is no such thing as too much. Being knowingly the presence of awareness is not something you *do* for a certain amount of time; it is what you always are!

My goal is to be always knowingly myself, but why is it I so often seem to miss the mark?

How can being yourself be your goal? You are already yourself! It's like saying, 'My goal is to breathe', except that being yourself is even more essential to you than breathing. You are already the self that is having the intention of being itself.

---

*William Blake, *The Marriage of Heaven and Hell* (c. 1790).

It's just that there are times when the thing that's supposed to transpire during meditation transpires, and there are times when it doesn't.

Nothing is supposed to transpire during meditation! The thing that is supposed to transpire during meditation is the one thing that is transpiring all the time. That is, the presence of your being. The fact of being aware.

Well, then I'm not meditating!

If meditation is something you do from time to time, it cannot be essential to you. It is added to you and then removed from you. Meditation is not an activity that you undertake in order to bring about a particular experience. The 'I' that you are is prior to the activity of meditation and cannot, therefore, depend on whether you are meditating or not. Meditation is to be knowingly the one you always and already are but may not have noticed due to your fascination with the drama of experience. Replace the word 'meditation' with 'being knowingly your self'. Ramana Maharshi suggested that the highest form of meditation was simply to *be*.

Meditation is what we *are*, not what we *do*. The separate self is an activity of thinking and feeling that we *do*; it is not what we *are*.

I think I have residues from decades of trying to meditate in exactly the wrong way.

Most of us do! But the years of meditation practice have not been wasted. They have brought you to this understanding. However, now that your previous practice has done its job, don't keep repeating it. Don't be like one who has finally arrived on a beautiful Caribbean beach after a long, arduous journey and keeps asking, 'Where shall we go next?'

It's not so easy to drop it. It feels like an ongoing process.

The idea that you have to drop something is itself part of the old residue of believing that meditation is a battle between one part of your mind and another. These old habits are the remnants of the storm clouds that linger in the sky for a while after the storm. If you struggle with them, you simply perpetuate them. The sky never struggles with the clouds. Why should it? It is not implicated by them.

Your self or being is not implicated by the content of your mind, so why have an agenda with it? Just let the residues of this old conditioned activity slowly wind down in your welcoming but disinterested presence. Sooner or later, this residual effort will die of neglect and the peace that was lying dormant in the background of experience all this time will begin to emerge.

There are times when I can easily practise this, but sometimes either my feelings are so overwhelming or my life is so busy and stressful that it just seems impossible.

This is not about practising; it is about recognising what is always and already the case but has been temporarily overlooked. You cannot become what you already are; you cannot be what you are not.

Simply be aware of your being. The awareness of being shines in you as the experience 'I am' before what you are is coloured or qualified by experience. Simply be knowingly your self all the time, irrespective of your circumstances: not just when sitting quietly with your eyes closed at certain periods during the day, but when you're having lunch, going for a walk, talking with a friend, answering an email, and so on.

Don't make a distinction between everyday life and meditation. Even when you go to sleep at night, feel that you remain resting in and as your being. In fact, in deep sleep, you don't really fall asleep; the world falls asleep in you.

Meditation is simply what we *are*, and what we are never leaves us. It is the only thing (which is, of course, not itself a 'thing') that cannot be separated from us. We take our self with us wherever we go.

If I am depressed, *I am*. If I am lonely, *I am*. If I am agitated, *I am*. If I am in ecstasy, *I am*. Whatever I am experiencing or feeling, *I am*. Allow the awareness of being to shine through your experience irrespective of its contents. Then you will find yourself at peace all the time.

CHAPTER SIX

The Ultimate Prayer

Accept, Lord, this my emptiness,
and so fill me with Thyself.

FRANCES NUTTALL

INTIMATE, IMPERSONAL, INFINITE BEING

When we, awareness, lose our self in or become mixed up with the content of experience, we seem to acquire its qualities. The clear luminosity of our being is dimmed or endarkened by experience.

However, just as the screen is never really veiled by a movie but only seems to be obscured due to the absorption of our attention in the drama, so our being is never really eclipsed by experience but only seems to be concealed, due to the exclusive focus of our attention on the content of experience.

And just as one who is lost in a movie may temporarily take on its mood, becoming sad if the scene is sad or scared if it is frightening, so we lose our self in the drama of experience, becoming mixed up with its content and seeming, as a result, to become conditioned or qualified by it.

Instead of experiencing our thoughts flowing through us like birds in the sky, we feel 'I *am* my thoughts'. The experience of agitated thoughts becomes the feeling 'I *am* agitated'. We allow our colourless being to be coloured by thoughts.

Instead of experiencing afflictive emotions like clouds passing slowly through the sky, we feel 'I *am* my emotions'. The feeling of sadness becomes 'I *am* sad'. The feeling of tiredness becomes 'I *am* tired'. Instead of experiencing sensations of the body like slowly moving clouds passing through us, we feel 'I *am* the body'. What we *are aware of* becomes, or seems to become, what we *are*.

In this way, our being is mixed with the content of experience and seemingly qualified or conditioned by it. The awareness of being is coloured or obscured by the awareness of experience.

The familiar experience of our self to which we refer when we say 'I am' becomes the belief and feeling 'I am this' or 'I am that'. Our unlimited, aware being becomes, or seems to become, a temporary, finite self or ego and, as a result, our innate peace and joy is veiled. It is this veiling of our being that is responsible for our suffering. The happiness we *are* becomes the happiness we *seek*.

THE DIVINE NAME

When we feel 'I am tired', 'I am lonely', 'I am depressed', 'I am stressed', and so on, most of us emphasise the feeling of tiredness, loneliness, anxiety or stress and neglect our self. Our being becomes mixed up with the tiredness, loneliness, anxiety or stress and seems, as a result, to be veiled by it.

On another occasion we may think, 'I am reading', 'I am walking' or 'I am eating', thereby mistaking an activity that we *do* from time to time for what we always and essentially *are*. Or we say, 'I am a mother or a father, single or married, a doctor, artist or gardener', and thus allow our being to be qualified or conditioned by a relationship.

All that is necessary is to relax or soften the focus of our attention from the feeling, activity or relationship and become aware of our self or being, the 'I am' aspect of experience.

In fact, we don't *become* aware of our being; our being is always aware of itself. But having lost itself in the feeling, activity or relationship, it *seems* to lose touch with itself and, therefore, appears to return to or become aware of itself.

To initiate this process, it is only necessary to take the thought 'I am' and stay with it, allowing it to invite us into the depths of our own being. The thought 'I am' is, as such, like the golden thread of Ariadne in Greek mythology. If we follow it, it will lead us out of the labyrinth of experience and return us to our being, where the peace and joy for which we long resides.

The *formulation* 'I am' is a conceptualisation of the *experience* 'I am', the awareness of being. It is like an image *of* the screen *on* the screen. As long as it is not qualified by experience, 'I am' refers directly to intimate, impersonal, infinite, self-aware being.

It is for this reason that 'I am' is said to be the divine name. It is a beacon *in* the mind of the reality that lies *behind* the mind and is, at the same time, the very *essence of* the mind. To abide in the 'I am' is the highest form of prayer.

THE SOUL, THE WORLD AND GOD

I have always thought of God as being at an infinite distance from myself. You seem to be suggesting that what is traditionally referred to as God is our very own being. Is that right?

Many of us intuitively feel that there is a reality behind the visible universe which the finite mind, due to its limitations, cannot know. However, believing ourself to be an individual person, we project this greater reality at an infinite distance from us, thereby satisfying our intuition that it is impersonal and unlimited but neglecting its intimacy. After all, we as a person emanate from the universe, and therefore, whatever is the ultimate reality of the universe must also be the ultimate reality of ourself. In this way, we emphasise its transcendence at the expense of its immanence.

Thus, the conventional idea of a creator God, beyond the world and at an infinite distance from ourself, is the inevitable corollary of the belief in ourself as a temporary, finite, independently existing entity. Instead of sinking deeply into our own being, discarding everything that is not essential to it, until its impersonal, unlimited but utterly intimate essence is revealed, we project God beyond the universe and then enter into a relationship of prayer and devotion to that God. The unity of being becomes the individual self or soul, the world and God.

To better understand this, imagine an actor, John Smith, playing the part of King Lear in Shakespeare's play. It is as if King Lear, believing himself to be the king of England, the father of three daughters and at war with France, intuits the presence of John Smith but, unable to find him in his own experience, projects him at an infinite distance from himself and then begins to search for him, entering into a relationship of devotion and supplication with him without realising that he is, in fact, his very own being.

This exoteric practice of prayer attenuates the ego or sense of separation, at least to a degree, and for this reason was considered a regulating factor in society for many centuries. However, in most cases, the sense of being a separate individual remains intact, and is even enhanced by its association with its particular image of God.

Being a projection of the mind, this idea of God must share its limitations. It is, as such, not so much that God 'made man in His own image', although that is true in another sense, but that man conceived God in his own image. Such a God must always be a product of the limited point of view of the mind that projects it, and thus is always in danger of becoming an idea in the service of the ego.

The egoic appropriation of the divine paves the way for individuals and nations to act out their beliefs and prejudices while claiming to be inspired and sanctioned by God. In this way, religion may cease to be a unifying principle in society and become a source of division, conflict and hostility.

Having said that, just as meditating on an object such as a mantra or the breath may be a prelude to the mind's subsidence in its source, likewise our devotion to an external God may be a preparation for the dissolution of our longing in its source of pure love.

And even after the traditional distinction between self and God has dissolved, the love that is the inevitable consequence of this dissolution may well continue to express itself in dualistic terms. Indeed, some of the finest poetry that has ever been written is couched in traditional dualistic language, although much of it bears the unmistakable signature of one whose sense of self has completely dissolved in God's being.

ABIDING AS 'I AM'

Just as the highest form of meditation is not the directing of attention towards an object, however refined that may be, but the immersion of attention in its source of pure awareness, so the highest prayer or the ultimate gesture of devotion is not a movement of our longing towards the beloved but the subsidence of our longing in its source of pure love. In the words of a sixteenth-century Italian monk, 'Lord, Thou art the love with which I love Thee'. It is the baptism of becoming in the ocean of being.

When attention is divested of its object, it stands revealed as pure awareness; when devotion is relieved of the beloved, it stands revealed as love.

Just as one who practises meditation must, at some point, relax the fierce discipline of attention and come to rest in and as the presence of awareness, the same is true for one on a path of devotion. The apparently separate subject of experience who once longed to merge with the object of her devotion now realises that she must abandon it and subside in the source of pure love from which her devotion arises.

Thus it is said, 'In the existence of your love, I become non-existent.'* On both paths, our efforts have brought us to a threshold beyond which they cannot pass.

At some point there is a shift or a conversion in our understanding: what appears from the perspective of a separate self to be the effort we make towards the object of our longing is, in fact, the subject of our longing attracting us into itself.

Our longing is only the veiling of love. What we, as an apparently separate self, experience as effort is, in fact, the gravitational pull of grace. All desire is the attraction of love.

For this reason, the ultimate prayer is to take the name 'I am' and lose oneself in its referent, abiding as that. In this abidance, our being is divested of the qualities and limitations that it acquires from experience and stands revealed as intimate, impersonal, infinite being.

Just as we take off all our clothes before going to bed at night, revealing our naked body, so, in the practice of prayer, we discard everything that is superfluous to us, leaving naked being revealed. The person has dissolved, leaving only impersonal, infinite, utterly intimate being. Thus, the art of prayer is to abide as 'I am'. It is the practice of the presence of God.

*   *   *

When I first heard about my true nature of being aware or awareness itself, it was easy and natural to reside there, but now the old habits of thinking and feeling have returned and I find myself going back and forth. How can I stay in awareness?

When you say, 'How can I stay in awareness?' you are taking yourself to be something other than awareness, such as a body or a mind. Awareness is considered something that you must approach, rest in for a period of time and then leave. This 'something other than awareness' is the bundle of thoughts, images, feelings, sensations and perceptions that constitute the ego or separate self that most people believe and feel themselves to be, and around whom their activities and relationships revolve.

*Jelaluddin Rumi, 'I Am Yours', The Love Poems of Rumi, translated by Fereydoun Kia, edited by Deepak Chopra (Harmony, 1998).

One of the activities of this apparently separate self is to undertake a spiritual practice such as meditation in order to cease being a separate self, with the suffering that inevitably attends it, and become open, empty, inherently peaceful awareness. However, such an activity simply perpetuates the separate self at its origin, which is why it is so frustrating.

So is there nothing I can do?

There is nothing that you, awareness, need to do to be yourself. You are already always only yourself. However, if we believe and feel ourself to be a separate self, then we are already doing something. What are we doing? Seeking peace and happiness in objective experience.

So what can I do?

Investigate the 'I' on whose behalf the search for peace and happiness arises. That is, turn your attention upon yourself and investigate who you really are, and in this way bring yourself back to the experiential understanding that you always and already are the awareness that you seek. All the peace and happiness you long for resides there.

It is easier said than done.

No, it is easier done than said! It takes but a moment to ask yourself who you really are and allow that question to reveal the ever-present awareness that is your essential, irreducible nature behind and within all experience. There is nothing complex about this. We know our self more intimately than we know any other thing. Even our most treasured thoughts and feelings are but strangers to us compared to the familiarity and intimacy of our own being.

Know yourself as the fact of being aware or awareness itself rather than a continuous flow of thoughts, images, feelings, sensations and perceptions. It is true that when any of these are present they *are* you, in the sense that they are made out of the awareness you are. But that is not *all* you are. They are ripples on the surface of your being. None of them define you or are essential to you.

Mind is always in movement. No movement, no mind. But what about awareness? Awareness is always just awareness, colouring itself in the form of the mind or remaining in its uncoloured condition. But irrespective of whether awareness is colouring itself as experience or resting colourless, does awareness ever leave itself and then come back to itself? Does awareness ever ask the question, 'What practice do I need to undertake in order to know myself?'

What does awareness have to do to be itself? Does it have to undertake any activity in order to maintain itself, or is it always effortlessly simply being itself? What kind of experience could prevent awareness from being itself? What kind of experience could prevent awareness from being aware? Is not awareness effortlessly being aware now?

What kind of a movie could prevent the screen from being the screen? Likewise, what kind of experience or activity could make awareness more aware than it already is? Does anything that takes place in a movie add anything to or remove anything from the screen? Similarly, does anything that takes place in experience add anything to or remove anything from your self, awareness? Can you feel the freedom that is your original nature and that needs nothing from experience?

I guess it's more about not being so identified.

But who has to be less identified? There is no separate self to be identified or not to be identified. There is awareness all alone or awareness colouring itself with its own activity, that is, awareness simply resting in and as itself or appearing in the form of experience.

See clearly that knowing, being aware or awareness itself is your *nature*. It is who you *are*, not what you might *become*. Let this be your new default felt understanding. It is not something you can work towards. There is no separate, independently existing 'you' who could become or work towards awareness. There is just awareness and its own activity.

And even when awareness is colouring itself in the form of thoughts, images, feelings, sensations and perceptions and seeming, as a result, to be a person, it is still not identical to any of these, just as a screen is never identical to any of the objects or characters in the movie. Awareness is always only ever identical to itself, for there is nothing in itself other than itself with which it could be either identified or unidentified.

So there is just the recognition of that?

Yes, there is just the recognition of that. And who is it that would recognise awareness? Only awareness is aware, and therefore only awareness is aware of itself or, indeed, aware of any other apparent thing.

But I still find experience distracts me from my true nature.

The drama of experience may retain the capacity to veil your true nature for some time, and therefore there may be a feeling of back-and-forth for a while. However, just as the movie loses its veiling power in time and, as a result, the distinction between the screen and the movie fades, so experience loses its ability to conceal awareness and, as a result, the distinction between awareness and experience diminishes and the conflict between them ceases.

At that stage there is no longer any back-and-forth, because it is all awareness wherever you go and whatever you experience. At that point meditation is life and life is meditation. We may still choose to sit quietly with our eyes closed for some time to rest in being, but we would not essentially be doing anything different from what takes place in the activities of everyday life.

* * *

I'm wondering about the balance between doing and non-doing, because I feel I need to make an·effort, yet at the same time I feel that non-doing is actually allowing me to step back more into who I truly am.

If it seems, to begin with, that an effort is required to be aware of your own being, then make the effort. First investigate your essential nature and then stand knowingly as that. Don't superimpose the idea of non-doing on yourself.

In time, it will be clear that you cannot make an effort to be what you always and already are. Indeed, it would only be necessary to make an effort to be something you are *not*, such as a separate self. That is why it is so exhausting to be a separate self! If I were to ask you to stand up now and take a step towards yourself, how much effort would you have to make?

None!

Yes! Any effort would only seem to take you away from yourself, although even that is not true, because wherever we are, we *are!* The same is true of meditation, which simply means to be knowingly our self rather than mistaking our self for a cluster of thoughts, images, feelings, sensations and perceptions.

However, if we feel that we are something *other* than this open, empty, inherently peaceful and unconditionally fulfilled presence of awareness, then we should make the effort to investigate our self, recognise our self and then be that knowingly.

All that then remains is to establish our self as that in all circumstances and to realign every aspect of our life with this felt understanding.

CHAPTER SEVEN

The Silent Presence of Awareness

My silence, life returns to thee
In all the pauses of her breath.
Hush back to rest the melody
That out of thee awakeneth;
And thou, wake ever, wake for me!

ALICE MEYNELL

AWARENESS IS IMMANENT AND TRANSCENDENT

The understanding that we are the awareness that witnesses, knows or is aware of experience is the first great recognition. It is the first step on the path to rediscovering our innate happiness.

In order to arrive at this understanding, we extricate ourself from the content of experience. We distinguish the knower from the known, the experiencer from the experienced. We have not manipulated or rejected any aspect of experience; we have simply seen that no experience is essential to us.

However, awareness does not witness experience from a distance like an aloof observer. Just as an image does not exist at a distance from the screen upon which it appears, likewise no experience stands apart from the awareness with which it is known.

Imagine a magical television screen that is not watched by someone sitting on a sofa but has the capacity to watch the movie that is playing on itself. It is an *aware* screen. We, awareness, are like that. We are utterly, intimately one with any experience and, at the same time, free from and independent of it. Awareness is both immanent and transcendent.

This recognition is often accompanied by a great peace and joy. For so long we have been oppressed by our conditioning and history, weighed down by our circumstances and relationships, and now we have the first taste of our inherent freedom. It is a liberation from the burden we have unknowingly carried around with us all our life, which usually becomes heavier as we get older.

Now the burden lightens. Occasionally it is discarded wholesale, in one simple recognition that is so complete and powerful that no experience ever again has the capacity to veil the nature of our being. More commonly, as this understanding percolates more deeply into us, the accumulated burden of experience is gradually eased, and in its place a peace and lightness emerge from within.

Later on, we will further collapse the apparent separation between awareness and experience. However, for one who is lost in the drama of experience and has, as a result, mistaken their self for a bundle of thoughts, feelings, sensations, activities and relationships, it is first necessary to make the distinction between the two.

AWARENESS IS ETERNAL AND UNCHANGING

Having extricated ourself from the content of experience and recognised ourself as the presence of awareness, the next step is to explore the *nature* of the awareness that we essentially are.

The essence or essential nature of anything is the aspect of that thing that cannot be removed from it. Anything that can be removed from a thing is not essential to it. No movie is essential to a screen because the screen can exist in the absence of movies. No cloud is essential to the sky because the sky can exist in the absence of clouds.

All thoughts, images, feelings, sensations, perceptions, activities and relationships are continually appearing and disappearing in our experience. They are added to us and subsequently removed from us. They cannot, therefore, be essential to us.

However, there is one element of our experience of ourself that remains consistently present throughout all changing experience, namely, the fact of knowing, being aware or awareness itself. It is that to which we refer when we say simply 'I' or 'I am', before what I am has been coloured, qualified or conditioned by experience. It is the constant factor in all changing experience.

In fact, the presence of awareness is not constant in time; it is ever-present now. It is only said to be constant in relation to the impermanence of things. However, being limited, the mind has no knowledge of the eternal and, therefore, construes it in a way that is consistent with its own limitations. It conceives the ever-present as the everlasting.

However, if we refer directly to the experience of being aware, that is, if awareness refers directly to its experience of itself, there is no thought present and, therefore, no knowledge of time. In its own experience of itself, awareness is simply ever-present. It is eternal.

It is from the ever-present nature of awareness that experience derives its singularity. A typical movie comprises approximately 150,000 frames, but when we are watching it we don't think we are experiencing numerous images; we feel we are watching *one* movie. The movie derives its unity from the singularity of the screen.

Likewise, we are always having only *one* experience, from which thought abstracts and conceptualises what is referred to in Buddhism as 'ten thousand things'. What is it that unifies the apparently disparate elements of our experience? Awareness, the silent presence behind and within all experience.

The presence of awareness is not something that we *become*, although in almost all cases its recognition requires some investigation. It is simply our essential, irreducible nature or true self, the ever-present background of all changing experience.

Just as a person in a cinema watches a movie, enjoying the good and bad characters alike, so we, awareness, witness or are aware of the entire spectrum of experience, irrespective of its content. And just as nothing that takes place in a movie changes the basic nature of the screen, so nothing that takes place in experience changes our essential nature of pure awareness.

The screen upon which a horror scene appears is the same screen upon which a romance unfolds. The awareness that witnesses our most ecstatic moments is the same awareness that witnesses our deepest sorrow.

Awareness never changes; experience always changes. It is for this reason that each of us feels that we are now the *same* person as we were five minutes ago, five days ago, five years ago or when we were five-year-old children.

But what is it in us that truly remains the same? The thoughts, images, feelings, sensations, perceptions, activities and relationships that constitute 'me', the person, have changed innumerable times over the course of our lives. And yet we feel each of these experiences as 'mine', betraying our recognition that there is in us a stable principle *to whom* they happen or belong.

That stable principle is our self, the immutable presence of awareness that we essentially are.

It is easy to verify this in our experience. If each of us were to compare the content of our current experience with the content of our experience as, say, a five-year-old child, the two experiences would be entirely different.

If, however, we were to refer to the awareness with which our current experience is known, and we were to have done so as a five-year-old child, the awareness in each case would be identical, just as all movies play on the same unchanging screen, irrespective of their content. Nothing ever happens to awareness; it does not change, age or evolve. That is, nothing ever happens to our essential self.

Each of us has encountered innumerable experiences in our lives, some of which were painful and traumatic. Whilst these may have left residues in the deeper layers of our mind, which find their counterpart as subtle tensions and contractions in the body, nevertheless our essential being, the fact of simply being aware or awareness itself, remains unchanged and unharmed by them.

This also accounts for the fact that many of us do not feel that we are getting any older. In this case, our essential, changeless nature is shining through the cloud cover of experience. Little do we realise how accurate this intuition is.

One might argue that every time we look in the mirror, we are confronted with evidence of ageing. However, when we look in the mirror we do not see an image of our *self*; we see an image of our *body*. The awareness that perceives the image in the mirror is in exactly the same immaculate, untarnished, ageless condition as the awareness that saw the image of our face in a mirror as a five-year-old child.

The Zen master who demands, 'Show me your original face before you were born' is simply trying to evoke in us a direct, immediate recognition of the ageless, pristine, ever-present nature of our self.

AWARENESS IS SELF-AWARE

All experience appears to or is known by awareness, but awareness itself never appears as an object of experience, just as the screen upon which a movie plays never itself appears as an object in the movie.

However, although awareness can never be known objectively, this does not imply that it is unknown or unknowable. If awareness were unknowable, we would not know that we are aware.

If someone were to ask us the question, 'Are you aware?', each of us would pause and then answer, 'Yes'. What is it that takes place in the pause between the question 'Are you aware?' and our answer 'Yes'? We become aware that we are aware. That is, we, awareness, become aware that we are aware.

If we, awareness, did not know the experience of being aware, we would have answered 'No' or 'I don't know'. But we are certain beyond any doubt that we are aware, and that certainty comes from our *experience* of being aware.

Now, who or what is it that has the experience of being aware? Only awareness is aware, and therefore only awareness can be aware of anything, including itself. Thus, our certainty that we are aware is *awareness's knowledge of itself*. In other words, awareness is self-aware, just as the sun is self-luminous.

Awareness's knowledge of itself is an utterly unique knowledge. It is the only knowledge that does not take place in subject–object relationship. In all other knowledge and experience, the object that is known – the thought, feeling, sensation or perception – is distinct from the awareness that knows it. But in awareness's knowledge of itself, the one that knows and the one that is known are identical.

I once heard a lecture on the nature of consciousness, given by a highly respected professor of philosophy at Oxford University. At one point he said, 'Some philosophers believe that consciousness can know itself; their ideas should be put in the rubbish'.

At the end of his talk, I asked him if he would agree that everyone in the room was presently having the experience of being aware. He agreed. I then suggested that whatever it is in each of us that is having the experience of being aware must, itself, be aware. He agreed.

When I then pointed out that whatever it is in us that is aware of being aware must, therefore, be awareness's awareness of itself, he simply dismissed the suggestion and turned away. In spite of his great erudition, he had overlooked the most obvious, intimate and familiar aspect of experience.

In the same way that the sun cannot direct the rays of its light towards itself as it does the earth or moon, and yet never ceases to illuminate itself, likewise awareness cannot be known as an object of experience, and yet it is never unknown. That is, it never ceases to know itself.

Awareness is self-aware *by nature* and, as such, cannot *not* be aware of itself. It is always aware of itself. It is aware of itself simply by being itself.

Awareness only seems to be unaware of itself because it is so accustomed to directing its attention, the light of its knowing, towards the content of experience. In doing so, it loses itself in experience and, as a result, overlooks or forgets itself. In other words, awareness's knowledge of itself is *obscured* by its knowledge of objective experience.

In the pause between the question 'Are you aware?' and our answer 'Yes', awareness does not *become* aware of itself. The question simply invites awareness to relax the focus of its attention from the content of experience and to 'come back' to itself.

*   *   *

Does everyone have the chance to become enlightened?

The question is based on a misunderstanding, namely, the belief that enlightenment is an extraordinary experience that may or may not be in reach of everyone.

That's true, but it is a misunderstanding that is almost universally shared!

That's also true! There are two reasons for this. The first is that Western culture has so profoundly lost contact with the simple understanding of our true nature that many people, at least until recently, turned to Eastern traditions for guidance on these matters. Although the recognition of our true nature – commonly known as awakening or enlightenment – is the same for all people, at all times and under all circumstances, the expression of it is inevitably coloured by the cultural conditioning in which it arises.

For Westerners, Eastern culture is, by comparison with their own, unfamiliar and extraordinary, and therefore the various expressions of the recognition of our true nature that arose in these cultures acquired an air of the exotic. India and Tibet may seem to have been extraordinary cultures from a Western point of view, but there is nothing extraordinary about the recognition of our essential being. In fact, our being is the most intimate, obvious and familiar experience there is, although, because it has no objective qualities, it is almost always overlooked in favour of objective experience.

The second reason, which applies to Eastern traditions as much as Western, is that the simplicity and directness of this recognition was often misunderstood and, as a result, became mixed with beliefs and practices that obscured and mystified the original understanding, conferring upon it an atmosphere of complexity which alienated many people.

But I have been exploring these matters for so many years and the recognition of my true nature seems as far away as ever.

Imagine that John Smith plays King Lear one night and Romeo the next. As King Lear he is miserable; as Romeo he is in love. Is any part of King Lear or Romeo's experience not pervaded by John Smith?

No.

Is the knowledge 'I am John Smith' less available in King Lear's experience than it is in Romeo's?

No.

Would the knowledge 'I am John Smith' be more available to King Lear if his relationship with Cordelia improved, or would the knowledge 'I am John Smith' be obscured for Romeo if he and Juliet fell out with one another?

No.

How far is the knowledge 'I am John Smith' from King Lear or Romeo? In other words, how much distance is there between King Lear or Romeo and John Smith?

No distance at all. They are the same person.

Exactly! There is no distance between anyone and their true nature.

Whether one is a saint or a sinner, healthy or sick, intelligent or unintelligent, wealthy or impoverished, makes no difference. The knowledge 'I am' – that is, awareness's awareness of itself – shines equally brightly in everybody's experience, irrespective of its content. So there is no question of enlightenment or the recognition of your true nature being 'far away'. How far is your self from your self?

No distance!

When you say, 'The recognition of my true nature seems as far away as ever' you are not referring to the recognition of your true nature; you are referring to an extraordinary event that you have perhaps read about in books and that you believe, should you be so lucky as to have such an experience, will relieve you of your suffering. As such, you are imagining that you are a separate person or self and that your true nature is an extraordinary experience that you, as this separate person or self, will one day find. Is John Smith an extraordinary experience that King Lear might one day attain?

No.

King Lear is simply a series of thoughts, images, feelings, sensations and perceptions that are added to John Smith and subsequently removed, but John Smith remains the same throughout. Likewise, your thoughts, images, feelings, sensations and perceptions are added to you and subsequently removed from you, whilst you remain the same throughout. What is that 'you', the one you call 'I'? Are you not already fully present now?

Yes, of course!

So-called enlightenment is simply the recognition of the nature of that 'you', the familiar, intimate, obvious, ordinary 'you' that you currently are. It is not a 'you' that you might find or become in the future, nor an extraordinary experience that you as a person might have, but the very 'you' that lies at the heart of your experience irrespective of its content, including your current experience. Therefore, it is not necessary to postpone this recognition to sometime in the future. The very idea of a search for your self is absurd. You are already that for which you are in search.

Nothing needs to happen to the self that you already and essentially are. It does not need to be stilled, purified, transformed or improved. Above all, it does not need to be enlightened. It is already the bright light of awareness that shines in the midst of all experience, be that a deep depression, a moment of ecstasy or the taste of tea. It just needs to be seen for what it is. That is, it just needs to see or recognise itself as it is, before it is coloured or qualified by experience. What is the nature of the 'you' – the one you call 'I' – that shines brightly in all your experience?

(Long silence)

Perfect! Stay in that silence and the memory of your eternity will emerge. Your self will remember itself: not the memory of an experience in the past, but the memory of something that is present in you now but which seems to have been obscured by the clamour of experience. Your self will wake up from the amnesia of experience and recognise or remember the self that it is and has always been.

That self – if we can call it a self – divested of the limitations that it seems to acquire from experience, is without limits, ever-present, immutable and imperturbable, and thus its nature is peace. It is devoid of any sense of lack, and thus its nature is unconditional happiness.

It feels neutral.

To begin with, by contrast with the objects of experience, it may feel neutral, but in time its innate peace will make itself felt. This is not a peace that is dependent upon what does or does not take place in experience, nor a peace that is *beyond* experience, but rather the imperturbable peace that is prior to and shines in the midst of all experience.

In time, that peace emerges from the background of experience and begins to pervade the foreground, progressively saturating experience with the feeling of sufficiency, fulfilment and contentment. That quiet, unconditional peace and joy is the hallmark of this recognition.

AWARENESS IS NEVER NOT KNOWN

If someone were now to suggest that we become aware of our breathing, we would relax the focus of our attention from these words and become aware of our breath. In fact, we do not *become* aware of our breath. We were already aware of it, although our awareness of our breath was eclipsed by our awareness of these words, our room and whatever else was commanding our attention prior to this suggestion.

Awareness is even more subtle than our breathing. It is the silent presence behind all experience which, like the breath, is always being experienced. That is, it is always knowing itself, although it often overlooks itself in favour of objective experience. So it would be more accurate to say that awareness's knowledge of itself is *partially* obscured by objective experience, and even then, only *seemingly* so.

Let us take another analogy to illustrate this. Imagine a woman just before she leaves home for work in the morning. When she thinks of herself, she thinks of herself as a woman. Now she goes to work at the police station. She changes into her uniform and starts her day's work with her colleagues in the office. She now thinks of herself as a policewoman.

In both cases, she knows herself as a woman. In the first case, her knowledge of herself as a woman is not qualified by any association or activity. In the second case, her knowledge of herself as a woman is qualified by her relationships and activities as a police officer. As a result, she now thinks of herself as a policewoman; she no longer knows herself as an unqualified woman.

Likewise, awareness never ceases knowing itself, because self-awareness is its nature. Its knowing of itself is simply mixed with the content of experience and so, in most cases, it does not know itself *clearly*. Awareness partially overlooks or forgets its knowledge of itself in favour of its knowledge of objective experience. That is the price it pays for experience.

Shantananda Saraswati used to tell a story of ten men who swam across the Ganges. Once on the other side, each man counted the party in order to ensure that everyone had crossed the river safely. Each man counted only nine.

A passerby, finding them distraught, enquired as to the reason, and they explained that one of their friends had drowned. Realising their mistake, he asked one of the men to count the group, being sure that he included himself at the end. 'One, two, three...' He arrived at 'ten' and, at that moment, each man realised that he had neglected himself.

Likewise, we tend to focus on thoughts, images, memories, feelings, activities, relationships, and so on, but we neglect our self, the silent presence of awareness in the background that peacefully witnesses it all. That is, awareness loses itself in the content of experience and, in doing so, overlooks or loses touch with itself. We pay for that neglect with our happiness.

To become aware of awareness does not require effort, any more than an effort was required for the tenth man to remember himself. All that is required is the *relaxation* of a previous effort, namely, the exclusive focus of our attention on the content of experience at the expense of our being.

As soon as this effort is relaxed, the presence of awareness shines by itself. It was always shining. It *is* always shining! However, if we are accustomed to losing our self in, or identifying our self with, the content of experience, it may seem, to begin with, that an effort is required to disentangle our self from experience, in which case we should make the effort.

In time, what previously seemed to require an effort will be felt as our natural condition. Thus, what may seem at first to be a practice, something that we as a separate person do, turns out in the end to be a non-practice. Only from the limited perspective of the separate self does what we *are* become something that we seem to *do*.

CHAPTER EIGHT

The Open, Empty, Aware Space

*It is precisely because there is nothing within the One
that all things are from it.*

PLOTINUS

*Is it enough to recognise oneself as the witnessing presence of awareness in the
background of experience?*

The recognition of awareness in the background of experience is, in most
cases, a necessary first step. However, it is important to understand that
the presence of awareness is not just the ever-present and unlimited *background* of experience but also the *medium* or the *field* within which all experience arises, in which it exists and into which it disappears when it
vanishes.

It is obvious, even from a conventional point of view, that thoughts and
feelings arise and exist within awareness. It is not so obvious that our experience of the body and the world, which is known only as a flow of sensations
and perceptions, also takes place in awareness.

If our attention travels from a thought to a sensation, for instance, the
tingling of our face, hands or feet, and from a sensation to a perception,
such as any sound that may be present in our environment, we do not find
our attention leaving one field in which thoughts appear and entering a second in which sensations appear, and then leaving the field in which sensations appear and entering a third in which perceptions arise. Our attention
is always travelling in the *same* field, the field of awareness.

As such, the relationship between awareness and experience is much more
intimate than that of an impartial witness to the objects of experience. At this
stage of understanding, awareness could be likened to a vast, empty, aware
space within which the objects of experience arise, in which they exist while
they are present and into which they vanish when they disappear.

At no point do we encounter, or could we ever encounter, anything that takes place outside awareness, just as a cloud never appears outside the sky. Even time and space, which we normally consider to be the vast containers within which all events and objects arise, are themselves experienced within awareness, the only place where any experience can appear.

Prior to the arising of experience, awareness is empty of all objective content, just as the space of an unfurnished room is empty of objects. In fact, it is on account of the emptiness of awareness that the fullness of experience is able to arise within it. If awareness were not empty, there would be no room for experience within it, in the same way that if an unfurnished house were not empty, there would be no room for the furniture within it, or if a screen were not transparent, it would not be possible for a movie to appear on it.

But my awareness seems to be confined and limited to my body.

Allow your attention to range freely over the entire spectrum of your experience and see if you ever encounter anything that takes place outside awareness. Would it be possible to have an experience that occurred outside awareness? See that your attention never leaves the field of awareness. Whatever it encounters is encountered *within* awareness. Indeed, attention itself is the focusing of awareness within itself.

Can you even imagine an experience that could take place outside awareness? Consider the extremes of experience: a near-death encounter, a vision of God, a drug-induced trip, a moment of ecstasy, intense pain. See in this way that all experience takes place in the space of awareness, the only medium within which it is possible for any experience to occur.

Notice that we are not speculating about an altered, expanded, mystical or enlightened state of awareness. Above all, we are not speculating about how awareness might become if we practise hard enough or meditate long enough; we are simply referring to our current, intimate, direct and ordinary experience of being aware.

Now see if you can find an edge or limit to the field of awareness within which your experience arises. We find a limit to everything that we know or perceive, but do we find a limit to the field in which that limited experience arises? And if we do not find any such edge or limit, what legitimacy is there to our belief that it is limited?

It is true that awareness permeates the experience of the body, and this gives rise to the feeling that awareness is located *in* the body. However, the room in which you are currently sitting is filled with space, but the space is not located in, nor limited to, the room. It is the room that appears in space, not space in the room. Likewise, the awareness which permeates the body and which, as such, gives rise to the feeling 'I am the body' is not generated by, located within or limited to the body. Your body is an appearance in awareness; awareness doesn't appear in your body.

In fact, awareness is not a vast, empty space. Having no form, it cannot be measured and, therefore, cannot legitimately be said to have an extension in any dimension. However, it is not possible to think of or imagine something with no dimensions; indeed, something with no dimensions is not 'something'. So as a concession to the mind, to enable it to think about or imagine awareness, we add a space-like quality, visualising it as a vast, empty field or space within which the entire content of experience appears. All that is required now is to remove space from this image of an aware physical space and what remains is dimensionless awareness.

I vividly remember the first time this became clear to me. Francis had often spoken of awareness as the space within which all experience arises, and although I had an intuitive understanding of this, I had never realised it in my own experience.

One morning, I was sitting with Francis and a small group of friends in his and his wife Laura's home in Northern California, when a dog began barking in the distance. I commented to him that it seemed obvious that the sound of the dog was taking place at a distance from, and outside of, myself. Francis suggested that I close my eyes and place my hands on the floor. I closed my eyes and slowly lowered my hands until they were resting on the carpet.

He then asked where the sensation was taking place. Was it taking place within awareness or outside awareness? I paused, referred to my experience, and realised that the sensation generated by my hands on the floor was taking place in exactly the same space of awareness in which my thoughts and feelings were occurring.

Before I had time to digest this insight fully, my understanding began to unravel, one recognition leading to another. I turned my attention again to the barking dog and realised that, if I referred only to my direct, immediate experience, without reference to thought or memory, it too was taking place within the space of awareness and at no distance from it.

It became clear that thought conceptualised 'the sound of a dog in the distance' but all I actually knew of this sound was the experience of *hearing*, and hearing was taking place *here*, within myself, that is, within awareness. There was no distance between myself, awareness, and the experience of hearing.

I had barely begun to ponder the implications of this observation when the thought arose, 'If awareness accommodates my entire experience, including the experience of the body and the world, what is the *nature* of the space of awareness within which these experiences are arising?'

A line from Milton's *Paradise Lost* came to mind, 'Thine this universal frame, thus wondrous fair: Thyself how wondrous then!'* The focus of my interest shifted from the sensation of my hands on the floor and the sound of the barking dog to the space of awareness itself. Awareness was turning its attention upon itself.

Until then I had believed and felt that awareness was located somewhere behind my eyes, looking out at the world, but now I was experiencing the body and the world within myself. It was obvious that awareness perceived the world *through* the body, but I had mistakenly presumed that this implied that it was located *in* and limited *to* the body.

The awareness with which the character in a dream perceives the world is not located in her body or, indeed, anywhere in the world which she perceives. It is, within the limits of the analogy, located in the dreamer's mind. Could the same be true of our experience in the waking state?

I looked for a limit or an edge to the field of awareness within which my current experience was appearing, just as I used to lie awake in bed as a child wondering how far physical space extended. However, the further I went, the more the edge or limit of awareness eluded me.

Like a scientist performing experiments to test the validity of a theory, I wanted to subject the possibility that awareness might be unlimited to the scrutiny of experience. Could I find or even imagine an experience that could take place outside of awareness?

*John Milton, *Paradise Lost*, Book v (1674).

Having said that, when I say, 'I looked for a limit or an edge', I do not mean to imply that I am one thing and awareness another. It was I, awareness, that was contemplating my experience of myself. In this way it became clear that in awareness's experience of itself there is no limit or edge.

ALL-ENCOMPASSING AWARENESS

As I, awareness, sank more and more deeply into my being, I felt that I was disentangling myself from thoughts, images, feelings, sensations and perceptions. As I did so, I felt myself expanding. I was no longer located in the head or chest. I was the vast, open, aware space in which everything was appearing.

It was both frightening and exhilarating: frightening because my habitual experience of being a finite self, located in and limited to the body, was rapidly dissolving; and exhilarating because I could not help but notice, in spite of the fear, the freedom and joy that accompanied this recognition.

It would be some time before I realised that I was not, of course, expanding. The belief that awareness was located within and limited to my head was simply being exposed and dissolved in the face of the evidence of experience. I began to feel what I had often read about in the traditional literature but had never been able to verify for myself: namely, that awareness extends beyond the limits of the body and the finite mind within which it seems to be housed, and encompasses the entire universe.

Just as my mind began to assimilate this understanding, it was followed by another. If physical space were emptied of all objects, we would have no experience of distance. Likewise, it is only in reference to the content of experience that awareness is considered a vast space. In our actual experience, that is, in awareness's experience of itself, there is no thought or perception and, therefore, no experience of time or space.

We all experience this vividly in deep sleep, when there is no activity of thinking and perceiving and, therefore, no corresponding experience of time and space.

With this understanding, the mind's attempt to conceptualise awareness comes naturally and effortlessly to an end. As a concession to the mind, it is legitimate to conceptualise awareness as an open, empty space, but in the absence of any need to do so, the mind falls silent and there is just the awareness of being, whose nature is unfathomable peace.

CHAPTER NINE

Peace and Happiness Is Our Nature

*I have seen what you want; it is there,
a beloved of infinite tenderness.*

CATHERINE OF SIENA

THE INHERENTLY PEACEFUL NATURE OF AWARENESS

Just as the physical space of a room cannot be agitated by anything that takes place within it, so we, awareness, cannot be disturbed by anything that takes place within us. Agitated thoughts, images, feelings, sensations and perceptions may arise, but the space-like presence of awareness within which they appear is itself not disturbed by them. Thus, its nature is peace.

And just as the space of a room is not *made* peaceful by modifying the behaviour of the people inside it, but is inherently at peace before, during and after their various activities, so our essential nature of pure awareness is always at peace, irrespective of the content of experience. It does not need to be purified, improved or stilled.

Whatever the content of experience that arises within it, awareness always remains the same: open, empty, allowing, undisturbed and without resistance. Awareness does not need to be made peaceful through effort, practice or discipline. It only need be recognised as such. That is, it only need recognise or know itself as such.

In fact, awareness is always knowing itself as it essentially is, but its knowledge of itself is mixed with its knowledge of objective experience and seems, as a result, to acquire its qualities. Just as a motionless screen seems to move when a movie begins, so we, awareness, seem to become agitated when we become entangled in the content of experience.

The inherent peace of awareness is not a temporary state of mind. It is the very *nature* of awareness itself and, as such, does not depend upon what does or does not take place in experience. It is prior to, and independent of, the content of experience and is always available in the background of experience.

It is the peace that 'passeth understanding', the peace for which there is no explanation in the content of experience. It cannot be caused; it can only be recognised. It cannot disappear; it can only be ignored. It is the context of the mind, not its content.

We usually first notice this peace in the background of experience and may only seem to have access to it in between our agitated thoughts and feelings, just as the screen only seems to become visible in between movies.

However, in time the content of our experience begins to lose its veiling power, just as a movie loses its capacity to veil the screen. As a result, the background of peace begins to percolate into the foreground of experience, which is in turn gradually and progressively permeated by it.

Awareness is not changed by the content of experience, but the content of experience is progressively changed by the peace of awareness.

HAPPINESS IS THE NATURE OF AWARENESS

Just as the empty space of a room does not stand to gain or lose anything from whatever takes place within it, likewise we, awareness, are not enhanced or diminished by any experience, however pleasant or unpleasant it may be. Awareness is always in the same pristine condition.

No experience adds anything to it or removes anything from it. As such, awareness has no vested interest in experience. It is utterly, intimately one with experience, open without resistance to it and yet, at the same time, needs nothing from it. It does not need to be fulfilled or completed by experience.

Awareness lacks or wants for nothing. As such, it is whole, complete, unconditionally fulfilled, content. From a human perspective this wholeness, completeness or absence of lack is felt as the experience of happiness. When we experience happiness we are literally experiencing our essential nature. Happiness is the taste of awareness.

Happiness is not a temporary state of mind, or even an emotion in the ordinary sense of the word. It is the ever-present background of all changing states and emotions. It is the *nature* of our self. As such, we cannot *know* happiness as an objective experience; we can only *be* it. Likewise, we cannot *be* unhappy; we can only *know* it.

Happiness is sometimes referred to as the ease of being, because it is to be found in the simple knowing of our own being as it essentially is.

I well remember the first time it became obvious that happiness is the very nature of my being. There was nothing extraordinary about it and it was not preceded by any particular experience. It just dawned on me. One moment it was not clear; the next moment it was.

The awareness of being is happiness itself. How could I have missed such an obvious truth? I looked back over twenty years of study and practice and realised that all the texts and teachings had been pointing to this simple recognition.

I recalled the innumerable attempts I had made in my life to secure happiness through objects, substances, activities, states of mind and relationships, and now, in the depths of my being, a quiet joy was revealing itself effortlessly.

Although this understanding would, over the ensuing years, be veiled from time to time by the old habit of seeking fulfilment in objective experience, it was never again completely eclipsed. The old habit had been dealt a mortal wound, and it was only a matter of time before it would dissipate, gradually giving way to an imperturbable peace.

This peace was not new, nor was it something extraordinary. It was familiar, like an old friend with whom I had lost touch and was now reunited.

It became clear that the answer to the question that had first formulated itself in my mind almost twenty years earlier, 'What is the source of lasting peace and happiness?', lay in the simple recognition of my own being. In short, it became clear that peace and happiness is the very nature of our self.

AM I READY TO KNOW MY SELF?

My experience is so overwhelming much of the time that I sometimes wonder whether I can ever recognise the presence of awareness.

Everyone is equally qualified to undertake this investigation and recognise their true nature, simply by virtue of the fact that they are aware. It is the very awareness with which you are currently aware of these words that has the capacity to soften the focus of its attention from the content of your experience, come back to itself and recognise its innate peace.

It is not even necessary to change or get rid of any element of experience, to still or silence the mind, to change negative thoughts into positive ones, or to transform unpleasant feelings. Whether we are deeply depressed, madly in love or simply drinking tea, we are aware of our experience.

The awareness that knows the experience of depression is the same awareness that is aware of the experience of being in love or the taste of tea. Even our most confused thoughts arise in the clarity of awareness. Even our darkest feelings arise in the luminous presence of awareness.

Is it possible that I'm just not ready?

This is a way of understanding, not a path of effort. Any effort would arise on behalf of a self that deemed its current experience insufficient and, therefore, in need of improvement. It would not arise on behalf of the true and only self of inherently peaceful and unconditionally fulfilled awareness.

This is a way of recognition and expression: the recognition of what is always already the case, and its subsequent expression or celebration in our lives. It has nothing to do with changing or improving a self which, when investigated, cannot be found as such. And yet, changes do take place in our lives as an inevitable consequence of this understanding.

All that is necessary is to cease being exclusively fascinated by or lost in the content of experience and to return to our self. Strictly speaking, we do not even need to return to our self. When we get undressed at night, we do not return to our naked body. It is simply revealed. Our naked body was there all along, underneath our clothes.

Likewise, our inherently peaceful and unconditionally fulfilled being is present behind, and in the midst of, all experience. All that is necessary is to relax the focus of our attention from the content of experience and our being will shine by itself. It is, as such, a relaxation of effort, not a new effort.

This kind of happiness seems out of reach for ordinary people.

No special qualifications, abilities or circumstances are required to recognise the nature of awareness. No sage – the Buddha, Meister Eckhart, Lao Tzu, Ramana Maharshi, Anandamayi Ma, Jesus or any other – had privileged access to the fact of being aware or awareness itself.

They were ordinary people, like each of us, who simply had a deep desire to know the nature of their being. They understood that happiness was to be found only in their own being and were passionate about finding it there.

Nor does this recognition require special affiliation to any particular tradition or person. One who has recognised the nature of their essential being knows that it is not coloured or qualified by any particular tradition, although they may continue to operate within that tradition, emphasising its inner meaning rather than its outer form, for the benefit of those who have yet to understand its full meaning.

Will I know when it happens?

This recognition may take place in contemplative moments, between thoughts and activities or during them, just as an actress may recognise that she is not defined by, or limited to, the part she plays in between performances or during a performance.

We may not even notice that a specific recognition has taken place. We simply notice that the almost constant activity of negotiating experience for the purpose of seeking happiness has diminished, and in its place a causeless peace has arisen. Either way, our inherently peaceful and unconditionally fulfilled nature of awareness does not need to be liberated from the content of experience. Its nature is already such.

The recognition may be accompanied by a dramatic relaxation of tension in the body or agitation in the mind, but this should not be mistaken for the recognition of our true nature itself. It is just as possible that this recognition may be accompanied by the simple thought, 'Oh, of course, why didn't I see this before?'

In time, this understanding will have a profound effect on our thoughts and feelings, and our subsequent activities and relationships, but this may be subtle and take place over a long period of time, depending on the extent to which our character diverged from it to begin with.

In fact, the realignment of the way we think, feel, perceive, act and relate with this new understanding never really comes to an end. Previously experience eclipsed awareness. Now awareness shines in the midst of experience, and all experience is progressively pervaded by and saturated with it, until it is finally outshone by it.

CHAPTER TEN

A Belief in Separation

The birds have vanished down the sky.
Now the last cloud drains away.
We sit together, the mountain and me,
until only the mountain remains.

LI PO

If our essential nature is ever-present and unlimited awareness, what is the ego or separate self, and how does it arise?

The ego or separate self could be defined as the identification of our self, awareness, with the content of experience, or the mixture of awareness with the limited qualities of the mind and body.

In the next chapter we will explore how awareness seems to acquire the limitations of the mind, which in this context I refer to mainly as thoughts and feelings. In this chapter we will explore how awareness seems to be defined by, contained within and limited to the body.

In speaking of the body in this way, I refer to it in the conventional sense, as a physical object. This of course implies an inherent dualism between the mind and body which is not intended, and which breaks down upon further scrutiny, but it is the way that most people understand and feel the body and is, therefore, a good starting point for how the belief in separation arises.

To understand how the unlimited presence of awareness that we essentially are becomes, or seems to become, the finite self or ego, let us take the analogy of physical space again.

Imagine the physical space of the universe before it contained any galaxies, planets or stars. It is a vast, borderless, empty space. Now in your imagination add the quality of *knowing* or *being aware* to this empty physical space. It is now an *aware* physical space.

Prior to the appearance of galaxies, stars and planets, there is nothing in this aware space for it to know or perceive. It is pure, objectless, aware physical space, pure in the sense that it is devoid of any content or objectivity. However, simply by virtue of the fact that it is aware, it knows *itself*.

The aware physical space's knowledge of itself does not take place in subject–object relationship, for a subject can only exist in relation to a separate object and vice versa. Its knowledge of itself is, as such, unique. It knows itself just by being itself, in the same way that the sun illuminates itself simply by being itself. In this case, that which knows is that which is known, without any separate subject that knows or any object that is known.

I SIMPLY AM

Now let us imagine that we were able to have a conversation with this aware physical space. Just as, in everyday life, we tend to ask a person their name before any other conversation, we ask the aware physical space what it would call itself if it were to give itself a name.

'I', it replies, for 'I' is the name that anything that knows itself gives to itself. It is for this reason that everyone refers to their self as 'I'.

We now ask the aware physical space about its primary experience of itself. 'I simply am', it replies, surprised that such a self-evident fact of experience even requires mentioning. The knowledge 'I am' refers to the aware physical space's knowledge of itself before it is qualified by any other experience. And as, at this stage, there is nothing in itself other than itself, the knowledge 'I am' is the totality of its experience. There is *only* its awareness of being.

We now ask the aware physical space if it experiences any limitation or division within itself. However, having no experience of anything other than itself, it does not even understand the meaning of the word 'limitation' or 'division', and so remains silent.

'Do you have a size, shape, age, gender, location, weight or boundary?' we ask. Again, silence. The aware physical space has no knowledge or experience of anything within itself that would enable it to qualify itself in these, or indeed any, terms.

'Are you ever disturbed, restless or agitated?' we ask. The aware physical space refers to its experience of itself and, again, looks puzzled. Disturbance, restlessness, agitation? There is just its own endless, silent, motionless openness.

'Do you lack anything?' we enquire, already intuiting its silent response. No, there is just the fullness of its own emptiness. It is neither something nor nothing, for there are, as yet, no things with which it could be qualified or contrasted.

This absence of limitation, disturbance or lack does not need to be conceptualised, for there is nothing in its experience of itself with which to contrast these qualities. Later they will be referred to, from the perspective of human experience, as its innate freedom, peace and happiness, not a freedom, peace and happiness that are relative to their opposites but the absolute qualities of its own nature.

Fast-forward several billion years, to the twenty-first century. The same aware physical space is now populated with galaxies, stars and planets. One of these planets is the Earth, on which are situated innumerable buildings. We enter one such building and make our way to one of the rooms.

Now we ask the aware physical space *in the room* what its name is. 'I' it replies, for as always, 'I' is the name that that which knows itself gives to itself. Then we ask the aware space in the room about its experience of itself.

The aware space in the room looks around and says, 'I am small, square, limited, dark and confined. I am contained within these walls, defined by their shape and dependent upon them for my existence.' A hint of nostalgia in its voice betrays the faint memory of the distant past when it knew itself without any such limitation.

We suggest to the aware space in the room that in describing itself in this way, it is not actually referring to its experience of itself but rather to the qualities and characteristics of the room in which it seems to be located.

'Instead of looking at the four walls of the room, look at yourself', we suggest. The space in the room turns its attention away from the four walls of the room and gives its attention to itself. 'I am...' A long silence ensues. It cannot find anything in its experience of itself to add to its essential awareness of simply being.

The aware physical space in the room suddenly realises that the feeling of longing that has characterised it ever since it seemed to have been contained within the four walls of the room was not, in fact, a memory of its distant past. It was the recognition of its own essential, ever-present being – the aware physical space of the universe – filtering through the limitations of the room with which it had mistakenly identified itself, drawing itself back into itself.

The yearning to which it had become accustomed, as the almost constant backdrop of its experience, falls away as an inevitable consequence of this recognition, and its innate freedom and peace are immediately restored.

AN IMAGINARY LIMITATION

Let us relate this to the experience of being a separate self or ego. The relationship between our essential nature of ever-present, unlimited awareness and the separate self or ego which we seem to be is analogous to the relationship between the unlimited aware physical space of the universe and the apparently confined aware space in the room.

Just as the aware space in the room was the *same* space as the unlimited aware space of the universe, so the self of the separate self or ego is the *same* self as the self of awareness, albeit with an imaginary limitation attached to it.

Just as the aware physical space identified itself with the four walls of the room within which it seemed to be contained and, as a result, believed and felt that it was small, confined and limited, likewise we, awareness, become mixed up in or identified with the 'four walls' of the body within which we seem to be contained and seem, as a result, to become a temporary, finite self.

Instead of understanding that I, awareness, pervade the body and perceive the world through it, we believe and feel that I am contained *within*, limited *to* and generated *by* the body. As a result, the experience 'I am' is eclipsed by the belief 'I am the body'. This mixture or identification of unlimited awareness with the limitations of the body creates the illusory separate self or ego.

What is the separate self's relationship with awareness?

The temporary, finite self does not, of course, exist *in its own right*, any more than the aware space of the room exists separate from or independent of the aware physical space of the universe. It is simply a belief, albeit a persistent and powerful one.

Nor can we say that a relationship exists between awareness and the separate self or ego, because they are not two entities in the first place, just as the aware physical space of the universe and the space in the room are not two separate spaces. The latter is simply an imaginary limitation of the former.

Thus, the separate self or ego is an illusory entity whose reality is derived from ever-present, unlimited awareness and whose apparent limitations are deduced from the fact that it perceives the world through the body and seems, as a result, to be located within and limited to it.

The identification of awareness with the limitations of the body is the seed of the apparently separate self or ego on whose behalf most of our thoughts and feelings arise, and in whose service most activities and relationships are engaged.

Is it possible to live and act in the world without the feeling of being a separate self or ego? I'm afraid that if I let go of myself as a separate self I'll no longer be able to function properly or have relationships.

The real question is whether it is possible to live and act sanely, harmoniously and creatively in the world *with* the feeling of being a separate self or ego. The sense of being a separate self is responsible for only three aspects of our life: unhappiness on the inside, conflict between individuals, communities and nations on the outside, and the exploitation and degradation of the environment.

Feeling itself to be a fragment, the separate self feels incomplete and unfulfilled, giving rise to the almost constant activity of seeking and resisting. That is, the ego is the source of all psychological suffering.

And just as the aware physical space in the room feels itself as an independently existing space, cut off and separate from all other spaces in the universe, so the separate self feels separate from everyone else. The aware space of the room is, of course, the *same* space as all other apparent spaces, but it does not know this.

Likewise, the separate self or ego does not realise that it shares its being with all other people and animals, giving rise to the feelings of isolation, envy, greed, injustice, cruelty, and so on. As such, the ego is the main source of all conflict.

Lastly, the ego does not realise that, at the deepest level, it shares its own being not only with everyone but with everything. This belief veils the felt sense of oneness with all of nature, thereby enabling it to exploit, consume and degrade the natural world with no regard for the consequences.

Therefore, if we as individuals in particular, and as a society in general, wish to be at peace and to live happy, creative and fulfilled lives; if we wish to have harmonious relationships with friends, family and strangers, irrespective of whether or not we agree with their ideas; and if we wish to live in a harmonious and sustainable relationship with nature, one thing alone is required: to evolve beyond the sense of separation or ego.

CHAPTER ELEVEN

There Is Only One Self

Otherness for the One
is the One without otherness.

BALYANI

I understand that the ego is an illusion, but it seems absolutely real. It feels as if there are two selves in me. One is this illusory ego that governs most of my life, and the other is the presence of awareness that I get occasional glimpses of. If these two are really the same self, why do they feel so very different?

The reason that your sense of self feels very real is that there *is* something that is undeniably true about your sense of yourself. When I suggest that the separate self or ego is an illusion, I do not mean to imply that it is non-existent. An illusion is not something that is non-existent. It is something that *does* exist but is *not what it appears to be.*

All illusions have a reality to them. For instance, the landscape in a movie is an illusion but its reality, relatively speaking, is the screen. The water in a mirage is illusory, but light is its reality. The snake we believe we see in the twilight is really a rope. In each case, all we are actually seeing is the reality of the illusory object, albeit with an illusion superimposed onto it.

Just as the aware physical space in the room owes its reality to the unlimited aware space of the universe but borrows its limitations from the four walls of the room, so the apparently separate self or ego owes its reality to ever-present, unlimited awareness but borrows its apparent limitations from the qualities of experience with which it seems to be mixed or identified.

This is why everyone's sense of 'being myself' is absolutely and undeniably real. It's just that, in most people's experience, their sense of self is so thoroughly mixed with the content of experience that, whilst they always know their self to an extent, they do not know their self *clearly*.

YOU ALWAYS KNOW YOUR SELF

To better understand the relationship between the apparently separate self or ego and our true nature of pure awareness, consider again the actor, John Smith, who plays the part of King Lear.

John Smith lives a peaceful and fulfilled life at home. Every evening he goes to his theatre, puts on a costume, assumes a series of thoughts, feelings, activities and relationships and seems to become King Lear, without, of course, ever actually ceasing to be John Smith.

However, although John Smith always knows that he is John Smith, he sometimes becomes so absorbed in, or identified with, the thoughts, feelings, activities and relationships of the part he is playing that he forgets or over-looks himself. He loses himself in his own creativity and, as a result, his knowledge of himself as John Smith is temporarily obscured by the belief and feeling that he is King Lear.

King Lear is not a person in his own right, so even the belief 'I am King Lear' is really John Smith's knowledge of himself, albeit coloured by the character of King Lear. In other words, there are not two people, John Smith *and* King Lear. There is *one person*, either revealed as John Smith or concealed as King Lear.

As such, King Lear is an *imaginary* person, an *illusory* self, created by the mixture of the very real person, John Smith, with certain thoughts, feelings, activities and relationships. However, from his own perspective, King Lear believes and feels that he is a real person, and he suffers accordingly. King Lear is right to feel that he is real, but he wrongly attributes that reality to himself as an independently existing person, forgetting that his sense of him-self is derived solely from the reality of John Smith. John Smith is, as such, the reality of the illusory person King Lear.

In the same way, the unlimited awareness that we essentially are becomes mixed up in, or identified with, the content of experience – thoughts, feelings and sensations – and seems, as a result, to acquire their limitations.

Just as John Smith 'clothes' himself in thoughts, feelings and activities and seems, as a result, to become King Lear, so we, awareness, 'clothe' ourself in experience and seem to become a temporary, finite self.

The temporary, finite self that we seem to be feels very real because it *is* real. Its reality is ever-present, unlimited awareness. All that is unreal or, more accurately, illusory about it are the limitations we ascribe to it. These limitations are imaginary. They are superimposed by thought onto the reality of our self.

Suggesting that you get 'occasional glimpses' of your true nature is like suggesting that King Lear gets occasional glimpses of John Smith. It is not King Lear who has glimpses of, or comes to know, John Smith, for John Smith is the only person present.

John Smith is always knowing himself, but his knowledge of himself is mixed with certain thoughts, feelings, activities and relationships, and therefore he ceases to know himself *clearly*. He knows himself partially, for even his belief in himself as King Lear is really his knowledge of himself as John Smith, albeit veiled or dimmed.

Likewise, you always know yourself. That is, you, awareness, always know yourself, but your knowledge of yourself is mixed up with thoughts, feelings, sensations, activities and relationships and, therefore, you do not know yourself *clearly*. You have allowed yourself to become endarkened by experience. What is commonly referred to as enlightenment is simply the removal of your ignorance of yourself and the clear seeing of yourself as you essentially are, before you are qualified in any way by experience.

So there is no question of two selves, one either knowing or not knowing the other. There is *just* your self – ever-present, unlimited awareness – either partially veiling itself with its own activity of thinking, feeling, sensing and perceiving, and seeming, as a result, to be a temporary, finite self, or ceasing to veil itself and thus knowing itself as it essentially is.

THE PRICE OF NAME AND FORM

Does this mean that as long as I seem to be a separate self and have experiences, I will have problems and suffer?

Experience itself is not problematic; it is our identification with it that is problematic. There is nothing inherently troublesome for John Smith about assuming the character of King Lear. He does so for the sake of the play.

For instance, doing so enables him to have three daughters, become the king of England and go to war with France. However, it *is* problematic for John Smith to lose himself so completely in the character of King Lear that he forgets who he really is. His suffering does not begin with assuming the character of King Lear; it begins with the belief that he *is* that character.

Now imagine that, as the character King Lear, John Smith becomes so lost in the drama of his experience that he forgets to revert to himself at the end of the play. A colleague who comes backstage to congratulate him on his performance is surprised to find him miserable.

'Why are you so unhappy?' he asks, and in response, King Lear recounts his troubles with his daughters, his kingdom and the war with France. 'You are not miserable for any of these reasons', his friend remonstrates. 'You are miserable because you have forgotten who you really are! Who are you really?'

'I am the father of three daughters, I am the king of England and I am at war with France, to name just a few of my troubles!' King Lear protests.

His response is, of course, only partially true. In each of these descriptions he refers to his essential knowledge of himself as 'I am'. However, his knowledge of himself is mixed with the content of his experience. He has allowed himself to be qualified by his experience, and as a result he no longer knows himself clearly. This lack of clear self-knowledge is alone responsible for his suffering.

'No!' exclaims his friend. 'You have not always been a father or a king, nor have you always been at war. Who are you prior to these relationships and activities?' King Lear describes his thoughts and feelings, but again his friend reminds him that none of these are essential to him. They all continually appear and disappear in his experience, but he remains.

Without realising it, King Lear is travelling back through layers of his experience towards his essential self or being.

As his friend's questions continue, King Lear finds it more and more difficult to respond. Long silences replace his previously agitated thoughts and feelings, for he cannot find any words to describe the nature of himself. The more deeply he sinks into himself, the less he feels he is defined by the character of King Lear. Then, at some point, he comes to himself, remembers himself: 'I am John Smith!'

There is nothing extraordinary or mysterious about the recognition 'I am John Smith'. It is not some new knowledge that John Smith acquires. On the contrary, all that has happened is that his previous ignorance of himself has been removed. In fact, knowing himself as John Smith is the most intimate, ordinary and familiar experience he has. It was simply obscured on account of his immersion in, or identification with, the content of experience.

All of King Lear's suffering arises on behalf of himself, the one whom he believes is being disrespected and maltreated by his daughters. However, if he looks inside himself, he undoubtedly finds thoughts and feelings, but he does not find the mistreated man, the suffering self, on whose behalf they arise.

The actual person King Lear cannot be found. He does not exist as such. After tracing his way back through the layers of his experience, discarding anything that is not essential to him, there is the recognition 'I am John Smith' and, as a result, the immediate end of his suffering. In the absence of the person King Lear, his suffering simply cannot stand.

Of course, it is not King Lear who has the recognition 'I am John Smith'. There is no such person either to have, or not to have, the experience of being John Smith. From the illusory perspective of King Lear, it seems that he is exploring his true nature or practising self-enquiry. However, there is no such person or entity present either to practise, or not to practise, self-enquiry.

The person that John Smith *seemed to be* – King Lear – and the person that John Smith *really is* are the *same* person. The former is simply an imaginary, self-assumed limitation of the latter. There is only one person: John Smith concealed or John Smith revealed. The concealing of John Smith's true nature was the cause of his suffering; the revelation of his true nature is the restoration of his innate peace and happiness.

The same happens with our self, awareness. It is awareness itself that freely assumes the activities of thinking and perceiving, without actually ceasing to be itself. There is nothing inherently problematic about doing so; indeed, it enables experience to take place.

Without 'clothing' itself in the activities of thought and perception, awareness would not be able to perceive or participate in the world. However, this comes at a price: in so doing, the formless, unconditioned presence of awareness seems to become qualified by, and subject to, the limitations of experience. Awareness loses itself, or seems to lose itself, in experience.

This identification of the presence of awareness with the qualities of experience constitutes the separate self or ego around whom most people's lives revolve. The separate self or ego is, as such, a compound entity whose essence is the presence of awareness and whose personal, limited, separate qualities are derived from the content of experience.

All psychological suffering takes place on behalf of this apparently separate self or ego. That is the price that the nameless, formless reality of unlimited awareness pays for assuming a name and a form. Although the separate self or ego is an illusion, from its own perspective it seems to be very real, and it suffers accordingly.

Because the reality of the separate self is the true and only self of unlimited awareness, it is only necessary for the apparently separate self to investigate itself, discarding anything that is not essential to it, until its essential, irreducible reality of pure awareness is revealed.

Thus, the apparently separate self or ego who *seeks* happiness, and the true and only self of pure awareness whose *nature* is happiness, are the *same* self, partially concealed in the former, fully revealed in the latter.

*   *   *

If the separate self is an illusion, what sense does it make to suggest that it should engage in some kind of spiritual practice or investigation?

One could argue that it is meaningless to suggest a practice or method to an illusory self, for the self that seeks happiness is like a wave in the ocean in search of water. Indeed, one could even contend that any such practice would further substantiate its illusory existence.

This may be true from an absolute point of view. However, returning to our analogy, it is highly unlikely that John Smith would have disentangled himself spontaneously from his involvement in King Lear's character without the intervention of his friend. Therefore, as a concession to the illusory self of King Lear, it is legitimate, and indeed necessary, to suggest that he explore his true nature or practise self-enquiry.

Likewise, it is extremely unusual for our self, awareness, to spontaneously extricate itself from the drama of experience and recognise its own unlimited nature, not to mention abide stably as that, without some intervention in the stream of its experience.

Although the recognition of our true nature cannot be caused by any activity, or the cessation of any activity, of the mind, if we prematurely subscribe to the belief that there is nothing we can do to bring about the end of our suffering, and we do not engage in some investigation or practice, we will tend to remain immersed in a habitual cycle of seeking and resisting, punctuated by brief periods of peace or joy.

Therefore, as a compassionate concession to the apparently separate self or ego that most of us believe and feel ourselves to be, the religious and spiritual traditions elaborate practices or pathways which lead towards the recognition of our true nature. That is, they take us from the self we seem to be to the self that we essentially are, from suffering to happiness.

Some of these practices give the apparently separate self an activity to undertake, with the intention of gradually purifying it until it is sufficiently refined to merge into its source. Others attempt to undermine the apparently separate self by refusing to recommend any practice that could be appropriated by it and used to validate and substantiate its illusory existence.

Others, such as the approach suggested here, recommend going directly to the heart of the matter and investigating the self we believe ourself to be, thereby revealing its inherently peaceful and unconditionally fulfilled nature.

CHAPTER TWELVE

Who Is It That Suffers?

Let yourself be silently drawn by the
stronger pull of what you really love.

RUMI

If our essential nature is inherently peaceful and happy, why do we suffer so much?

Let us first make a clear distinction between physical pain, discomfort or danger and psychological suffering. Pain, discomfort and resistance to danger arise on behalf of the safety and well-being of the body. They are expressions of the body's innate intelligence to protect and preserve itself.

For instance, if we have a toothache, the pain is an intelligent signal that the body requires attention. If we are hungry, the mildly uncomfortable sensation indicates that the body requires nutrition. If our house is on fire, our resistance to the situation arises on behalf of our safety and those in our care.

By contrast, psychological suffering arises on behalf of the belief that we are a separate and independently existing self. Imagine, for instance, that someone says something and we are hurt by it. Who or what is hurt? The body is obviously not injured by the words. They do not harm our ears or our head. And the open, empty space of awareness is not hurt; the words sail through it like a bird in the sky, without harming it in any way or leaving a trace on it.

Yet something rises up in us between awareness and the body and says, '*I* feel upset'. Who is that 'I'? It is an illusory entity, the separate self or ego, on whose behalf all afflictive emotions arise. It is in response to the discomfort of such emotions that most people seek relief in objects, activities, substances, circumstances and relationships.

In this approach, we address the root of suffering. We attend to the self that is hurt rather than to the hurtful words themselves. If that self is seen to be an illusion, how can the suffering that arises on its behalf remain?

The suffering dissipates as a result of this clear seeing, and our innate peace and happiness, which was present all along but veiled by the emotion, is restored.

The Buddha clearly described this process in the Four Noble Truths, which state that there is suffering, it has a cause, there is the possibility of its ending, and there is a means by which this may be accomplished. Restated in the affirmative, this might read: there is happiness, it is our true nature, it may easily be found, and there is a simple and direct path to it.

THE ACTIVITY OF THE EGO

Let us return to the cause of suffering. The separate self or ego is an illusion. It is an apparent contraction or limitation of our true nature: the ever-present, unlimited presence of awareness with which all experience is known, in which all experience appears and, ultimately, out of which all experience is made.

This illusory self, feeling itself to be a fragment rather than whole, is always seeking to complete or fulfil itself through the acquisition of an object, substance, activity, circumstance or relationship. As such, seeking is the means by which the ego attempts to restore its innate wholeness.

Feeling itself to be a fragment, the separate self or ego always feels threatened and vulnerable. For this reason, it is always in a state of resistance or defence against anything that it perceives will endanger or diminish it.

This resistance and defence does not arise on behalf of the safety or well-being of the body. Its purpose is to protect or defend an illusory psychological entity. Criticising, blaming, judging, accusing and arguing are some of the many ways the ego protects and enhances itself, thereby validating and perpetuating its illusory existence.

Thus, seeking and resisting – desire and fear – are the two activities that define the separate self or ego. In fact, the ego is not an *entity* that seeks and resists; it is the very *activity* of seeking and resisting. Seeking and resisting are not what the separate self *does*; they are what the separate self *is*. They are the activity that inevitably attends the belief that we are a temporary, finite self.

To better understand this, consider the analogy of a rubber ball. In its natural condition, a rubber ball is in a state of equilibrium. If the ball is compressed, its natural state of equilibrium is disturbed and a tension is set up within it.

We could say that the 'memory' of the ball's natural state exerts a force on the compressed ball, whose purpose is to restore its original condition.

Likewise, being an apparent contraction of inherently peaceful and unconditionally fulfilled awareness, the separate self or ego is always in a state of tension. This state of tension is, by definition, always seeking to return to its natural condition of equanimity, openness and fulfilment.

Whether it does so by seeking objects, substances, activities, circumstances and relationships, or whether it is engaged in the same search via religious or spiritual means, it is, without knowing it, responding to the gravitational pull of happiness within its own being.

Little do we realise that it is not our self who is seeking happiness; it is happiness that is seeking our self. As Daniel Ladinsky interprets the Sufi poet Hafez, 'Ever since happiness heard your name, it has been running through the streets trying to find you'.* After all, the separate self is an illusion, and an illusion cannot do anything, let alone seek happiness.

What is considered from the illusory perspective of a separate self to be its search for happiness in the future is, in fact, the gravitational pull that awareness exerts on its own contracted form in an attempt to restore its natural, ever-present state of equilibrium, that is, its innate peace and happiness. We are the happiness we seek.

In the religious traditions, the gravitational pull that our own being exerts on its own apparently contracted, limited form is referred to as grace. As such, grace is not a special moment that is conferred upon us by some external deity. It is the continuous attraction of our deepest self, inviting us to return home to the peace of our being.

All psychological suffering is an extension of the two primary activities of seeking and resistance, which are, in turn, the outcome of the belief in being a temporary, finite, separate self. Suffering is, as such, the inevitable consequence of the overlooking or forgetting of our true nature, whose nature is happiness.

Happiness is the nature of awareness; suffering is the activity of the ego.

Seeking and resisting are the defining characteristics of the separate self or ego, and therefore the ego is always trying to escape from its current

*Daniel Ladinsky, 'Several Times in the Last Week', *I Heard God Laughing: Renderings of Hafiz* (Penguin Books, 2006).

experience into the past or future. Thus, the ego considers the now to be the cause of its suffering. Therefore, it is always trying to avoid it.

The ego is at war with the now. It is always seeking to replace or resist it. Seeking propels the ego into the future; resistance drags it into the past. It is for this reason that those in whom the activity of ego is very strong tend to live either in the future, in anxiety, restlessness or worry, or in the past, in regret, disappointment, resentment and nostalgia.

Of course, the ego (if we may continue to refer to it as an entity) does not realise that the peace and happiness for which it longs is its very nature and can only be found in the now, in the depths of itself. Ironically, it perpetually escapes from the now, the only place where peace and happiness can be found, into the past or future, the only place where suffering dwells.

In fact, the vast majority of our thoughts about the past and future arise solely to accommodate the separate self and its inherent rejection of the now. Meanwhile, the ego remains unaware that its search for peace and happiness is, in fact, inspired by the intuition of its own unlimited and ever-present nature.

THE VANISHING OF THE ILLUSION

I understand that the sense of separation is an illusion. However, it is such a strong feeling, and it seems almost impossible to get rid of it.

Any attempt to get rid of the separate self is predicated on the belief that it exists as such to begin with. Therefore, in the ultimate analysis, such efforts *substantiate* its apparent existence. The separate self perpetuates itself by trying to get rid of itself.

Trying to get rid of the separate self or ego is like trying to get rid of the snake that we believe is coiled up in the corner of the garage. Nothing we do to the apparent snake will get rid of it, because it is not there to begin with. The snake is simply a mistaken perception of the rope that can only persist as long as the rope is not clearly seen. The ego is like the snake; it is a mistaken perception of our true self, the unlimited presence of awareness.

Just as the snake is an illusion whose seeming existence disappears as soon as we see its reality, the rope, so the separate self or ego is an illusion which vanishes as soon as we see its reality, unlimited awareness.

Just as the aware space of the room is the *same* space as the aware space of the universe, just as the self of King Lear is the *same* self as the self of John Smith, so the 'I' of the ego is the *same* 'I' as the infinite 'I' of awareness, the only 'I' there is.

All our thoughts, feelings, activities and relationships are pervaded by the sense of 'being myself' or the sense of 'I'. In other words, each of us bears the memory of our true nature within us all the time. It shines in us as 'I'.

All that is necessary is to discern that 'I' clearly. That is, all that is necessary is for our self to know *itself* clearly, before it is coloured, qualified or limited by any experience.

This is what Ramana Maharshi meant when he said, 'When the "I" is divested of the "I", only "I" remains'. That is, when the 'I' of the apparent ego is divested of all the beliefs and feelings with which it has clothed itself, the true and only 'I' of inherently peaceful and unconditionally fulfilled awareness shines by itself.

So it is not necessary to have any agenda with the content of experience, and even less with the apparent ego itself. It is only necessary to discern the 'I' that shines brightly in the midst of all experience, and our innate happiness will be restored.

*   *   *

You mentioned once that we don't really age, but I certainly feel that I am getting older every day.

Ageing is a concept, never an experience.

It's a powerful concept!

No concept is powerful. Concepts are neutral; beliefs are powerful.

I don't just believe I'm ageing; I feel it.

What exactly do you feel is ageing?

My body!

All we experience of the body is a flow of sensations and perceptions appearing in awareness. Even to say we experience a *flow* of sensations and perceptions is a concession to the mind. At any moment, there is just the *current* sensation and perception.

How old is the current sensation or perception? Twenty-seven, fifty-two, sixty-eight years old? No! The current sensation and perception are just appearing brand new, fresh, now – not now, a moment in time, but now, the ever-present, bright, luminous, pristine awareness in which all experience arises and out of which all experience is made.

Even to refer to sensations and perceptions appearing *in* awareness is a concession. We do not experience sensations and perceptions appearing *in* awareness. There is just awareness and its own activity: awareness modulating itself in the forms of sensing and perceiving but never ceasing to be itself, nor becoming or knowing anything other than itself. As such, sensations and perceptions are not like fish appearing *in* the ocean; they are like waves and currents, movements *of* the water within itself.

Awareness knows nothing of time or ageing. The ideal of eternal youth has been downgraded by our culture to imply a body that looks perpetually young. To be eternally youthful means to know and feel oneself as ageless awareness.

But I experience time.

Awareness only knows now; the mind imagines time.

Experience conforms to our understanding of ourself. If we believe and feel that we are essentially a body, then we will believe that we are ageing and we will experience the body in a way that is consistent with that belief.

If we understand and feel ourself to be ever-present awareness, or the fact of simply being aware, before it is qualified by experience, we will feel that we are always the same ageless self. We will feel that we are always here and now, and that all experience flows through us without changing, ageing or harming us in any way.

I feel life's experiences are always changing me.

We *experience* numerous changes, but we, awareness, are changeless. We do not move through life's experiences; life's experiences move through us.

But I feel my life is a great journey.

The journey takes place in you; you do not take the journey. The time and space that seem to exist for the character in a dream do not exist for the dreamer when she wakes up. The entire dream is a movement of the dreamer's mind, but the dreamer's mind never goes anywhere. Our entire life is a movement of awareness, but awareness itself never goes anywhere. Awareness is eternally present now – not now, a moment in time, but the ever-present now, eternity. Awareness is always in the placeless place of itself, not a place in space but the dimensionless presence of its own being.

Some people seem to get more youthful and radiant as they get older.

Yes! In fact, many people feel that in spite of the passing years they are not really growing older. They increasingly have the feeling of being always the same person. Where does this feeling come from? It can only come from that which is always the same in us. What is that?

Knowing, being aware or awareness itself is the only element of experience that always remains the same. The feeling that we never get older or that we have always been the same person is an intuition of this truth. In fact, it is more than an intuition; it is the *taste* of our eternity, the taste of our ever-present, ageless, changeless, untarnished self.

The more deeply this is understood and felt, the more brightly the innate qualities of our essential, aware being shine through the character of the person, infusing the mind and body with its radiance and peace, and shedding its warmth upon those with whom we come in contact. In old age, as the mind and body of such a person fade, they become increasingly transparent to their being, which in turn progressively shines through all aspects of their experience. It is a blessing simply to be with such people.

But I am regularly in pain.

There may be intense sensations, but do not allow the intensity of a sensation to persuade you that you are a body, let alone an ageing one!

But I am unwell more and more often.

Does awareness ever say, 'I am sick'? Does the body ever say, 'I am sick'? No! It is the mind that claims, 'I am sick'. But even that claim is just a thought. Can a thought be sick? Can a sensation or a perception be sick? No! Sickness is, in the ultimate analysis, a concept. And this understanding is the ultimate healing: not a cure that will heal us in the future, but a cure that leads us directly to that in ourself which is already and inherently free of sickness and death, irrespective of the condition of the mind and body.

I do not mean to imply that it is not legitimate or appropriate to take relative steps to heal illness, but such steps should not eclipse the background of stillness and well-being against which all experience takes place. Ultimately, to be healthy means to be whole, unbroken, undivided and, therefore, without conflict or dissatisfaction. Don't try to become that; see that what you essentially are is always and already that. Make this understanding your lived and felt experience.

CHAPTER THIRTEEN

Our Innate Happiness

Thus the master travels all day without leaving home.
However splendid the views, she stays serenely in herself.

LAO TZU

HAPPINESS IS ALWAYS THE SAME

I understand clearly that peace and happiness is the nature of myself, but I have to admit that my happiness is very much dependent on my circumstances. When they coincide with my desires, I'm happy. When they don't, I suffer. So I feel caught between my genuine understanding and my undeniable experience.

Everyone has experienced periods of happiness in their life, and in most cases each occasion was preceded by a particular object, substance, activity, circumstance or person. When we were five years old, our happiness seemed to be caused by a trip to the seaside or the ice cream that our mother gave us. At age ten it was winning a competition or becoming friends with a particular person. In our teenage years, the happiness seemed to be caused by falling in love, a trip abroad or winning a game at school. Later on, in our twenties, it may have been our first job, a new home, getting married, starting a family, and so on.

In this way, a clear connection between happiness and the acquisition of a particular object or substance, or the experience of a particular activity, circumstance or relationship, was established early on in our lives. From this connection we concluded that happiness must be caused by objective experience, even if we didn't formulate it to ourself in these terms. This conviction would subsequently initiate and justify an endless and ultimately frustrating search for happiness in objective experience.

If we look more closely, we discover that the premise of this conclusion is far from true. To begin with, we notice that in every instance of happiness, the experience of happiness itself is *always the same*. The experience of happiness when, as a child, we won a competition at school, was exactly the same as the experience of happiness that we felt as a teenager upon falling in love, or as a young adult on getting our first job, or indeed at any time in our life when we felt happiness.

Happiness does not come in different flavours, although it may seem to be caused by different circumstances. Happiness itself is always the *same* experience, irrespective of its apparent cause. This observation alone should arouse our suspicion as to the causal connection between objective experience and happiness.

Our suspicion is confirmed when we notice that whoever or whatever may seem to make us happy one day may leave us indifferent the next, or may even, in time, make us miserable. The discarded toy that only a few days earlier gave the child such delight is quickly forgotten, or the intimate relationship that was once a source of such joy is now the cause of sorrow.

If happiness were really caused by an object, substance, activity, circumstance or relationship, then as long as one of these were present, happiness would be experienced. Conversely, the same must be true of suffering. If the same object, situation or person can make us happy one day and miserable the next, then none of these can itself be a cause of suffering.

If happiness were caused directly by objective experience, then certain experiences would make everybody happy. However, this is not our experience. If health were a source of happiness and sickness a source of unhappiness, all healthy people would be happy and all sick people would be unhappy. If wealth were a source of happiness, all rich people would be happy and the impoverished would be miserable. This is obviously not the case.

If one person is a gardener in California and it rains in August, she will be delighted. If another is a lawn tennis player in Oxford and it rains in August, he will be miserable. The rain itself is neither pleasant nor unpleasant. It has no inherent power to make us either happy or miserable. It is our inner disposition that confers on the rain the ability to cause happiness or suffering.

Furthermore, the *same* event can make one person happy and another person miserable *at the same time*. In a tennis match between Roger Federer and Rafael Nadal, everyone is watching the same game, but if Federer wins, half the spectators will be happy and half will be unhappy, and vice versa.

If the same event can simultaneously be the cause of happiness in some people and unhappiness in others, then the joy and suffering experienced cannot have anything to do with the event itself. It has everything to do with the attitude we bring to bear on the event, an attitude which does not arise in response to the current event itself but comes from our own past conditioning. From this we may draw a simple conclusion: nothing objective has any inherent power to cause either happiness or suffering.

Then why is it that our external circumstances seem to have the capacity to make us happy or miserable?

The fact that the fulfilment of a desire seems to bring about happiness does indeed suggest that objects, substances, activities, circumstances and relationships are its cause. However, the acquisition of any of these does not cause the happiness that we experience. Rather, it brings to an end the state of desire, the activity of seeking and resisting, that defines the ego or separate self.

In the absence of seeking and resisting, that is, in the absence of any impulse to escape the now, we find ourself at one with our current experience and aligned with the flow of the universe. We no longer separate ourself from the totality of experience as an independently existing entity that either likes its experience and wants to hold on to it or dislikes its experience and wants to get rid of it. As a result, our true nature of peace and happiness shines.

The happiness has not been caused by anything outside of ourself. It is simply the natural condition of our self, which previously was obscured by the activity of seeking and resisting and is now revealed.

When my son was six or seven years old, I gave him a pair of goalkeeping gloves for his birthday. He impatiently tore open the packaging, gazed at the gloves and exclaimed, 'Oh, I love getting new things!'

Without realising it, he had intuited that it was not the gloves themselves that gave him that moment of joy. It was their newness that had the power to put an end to the state of expectation – that is, the future – and bring him directly into the present.

And how do we escape the present and venture into the future? Through thought. For my son, the gloves temporarily put an end to thought, and in its absence, the presence of awareness lying just behind thought, and usually veiled by it, was experienced. That is, it experienced itself.

Had the gloves themselves been the source of happiness, then whenever he had the gloves with him, he would have been happy. Suffice it to say that this was not the case! For a few days the gloves retained their capacity to bring him into the now, that is, to the experience of happiness, and for as long as this lasted, he continued to enjoy them. But in time they lost this capacity and, although he continued to use them, they were no longer a source of happiness.

Most of us will be able to relate to this story. We need only substitute for the goalkeeping gloves the object, substance, activity, circumstance or relationship of our choice. Believing that the object itself was the cause of the happiness we previously experienced, the mind sets out in search of another such object or experience, thereby perpetuating an endless cycle of seeking and disappointment, punctuated by fleeting intervals of happiness.

In this way, apart from relatively brief periods of respite, most people's experience is characterised by the state of seeking and resisting. As a result, their innate peace and happiness remains, for most of the time, an unrealised potential.

SEEKING AND RESISTANCE

But I don't desire just any old object, circumstance or relationship to put an end to my dissatisfaction. My desires are very specific. If they weren't, anything or anyone would do. Alas, this is not the case!

External circumstances seem to have the power to cause happiness or unhappiness only to the extent to which they coincide with the conditioned layer of likes and dislikes lying in the depths of our mind. This layer of individual preferences lies between the background of awareness and the foreground of objects and people, and constitutes a filter through which our experience is mediated.

This intermediary layer of subliminal feelings is triggered by our experience of the world and, in turn, triggers the activity of seeking and resisting. If our experience of the world does not activate this layer of likes and dislikes, there is no inclination in us to resist the current experience or to seek a new experience.

For instance, if we were neither a gardener in California nor a lawn tennis player in Oxford, we would have no pre-existing attitude towards the rain and would, therefore, neither seek it when absent nor resist it when present. If we did not have a preference for Federer or Nadal, the outcome of their match would not have the capacity to make us happy or sad. If my son did not love football, the gloves would have had no power to elicit happiness.

In the absence of preferences and the activity of seeking and resisting they generate, we are one with our current experience and, as a result, our innate happiness is felt.

Around about the same age my son received the gloves, I took him to his first football match. Just before the game began, I asked him which side he wanted to win. He looked at me with a puzzled expression, as if it were a foolish question, and replied, 'Whoever scores the most goals'.

It was one of those disarmingly simple and uncannily wise comments that children of a certain age sometimes make. Such comments are informed by an innocent and luminous intelligence which has not yet been moulded by rational thought.

In relation to the football match, my son's mind had not been conditioned with preferences, and therefore he did not bring the past to bear on his current experience. There was no resistance in him to the current situation because he did not have a preconceived idea in his mind as to how the game should unfold. His state of mind was one with the current situation in whichever direction it flowed. He simply wanted whoever was winning to win! He wanted whatever was happening to happen.

In time, of course, my son would grow up to overlook this understanding. However, it attests to the intelligence that is the essence of each of our minds and that, although obscured in most cases, is always available behind the layers of conditioned thought and feeling.

The same innocent, luminous intelligence was expressed some fourteen hundred years ago by the Third Patriarch of Zen, Seng-Ts'an. His famous poem *Hsin Hsin Ming* – which could be translated as *Trusting the Nature of Awareness* – is one of the pre-eminent texts of the Zen Buddhist tradition:

To be at peace and content is not difficult for those who have no preferences. When likes and dislikes are not present everything becomes clear
and simple. Make the smallest distinction, however, and you will be exiled
from the realm of eternal happiness which is your birthright. If you wish
to be happy and at peace, then hold no opinions for or against anyone or
anything. To set up what you like against what you dislike is a conditioned
habit of the mind. It is a recipe for misery. When we allow things to be as
they are, things allow us to be as we are, and the peace and happiness that
is our nature emerges effortlessly.*

UNCONDITIONAL OPENNESS

Happiness is always present within us, latent but obscured by our resistance
to the current situation. This resistance is, in turn, activated on behalf of the
subliminal layer of our conditioned likes and dislikes. Indeed, we do not
seek any object, substance, activity, circumstance or relationship for its own
sake but rather to satisfy the demand implicit in our preferences.

When this demand is met, our resistance to the current situation comes to
an end. We become aligned with our current experience rather than in opposition to it. In that alignment with what is, our innate happiness shines forth.

A sane person is one who does not wait for their circumstances to align
with their preconceived ideas of how they should be. Their happiness is
prior to, and independent of, the content of experience. They do not allow
experience to determine their happiness; they bring their happiness to experience, in the form of unconditional openness to whatever it is they are
experiencing.

I once heard a story of a ninety-two-year-old woman who, when her hus-
band of sixty years passed away, registered to move into a care home. On ar-
rival, she was greeted and taken to see her new room. As they entered the
lift, she said to her carer, 'I love it!' 'What?' enquired the carer. 'The room',
she said. 'But you haven't seen it yet', the carer responded, perplexed. 'That
has nothing to do with it!' the elderly woman replied.

To search for happiness in objective experience is fundamentally flawed.
It is to court misery. One who sees this clearly withdraws their expectation

* This is my own rendition of *Hsin Hsin Ming* by Seng-Ts'an, compiled from numerous translations.

and demand that people and circumstances be a source of happiness. To search for peace and happiness in objective experience is to set oneself up for failure and disappointment and to sow the seeds of conflict in relationships.

All psychological or emotional suffering arises on behalf of our resistance, and our resistance is something that rises up within us. No person or circumstance imposes suffering on us; we do it to ourself. Happiness is what we *are*; unhappiness is the activity of seeking and resisting that we *do*.

Unhappiness always has a cause – namely, the frustration of our expectations and the subsequent activity of seeking and resisting – whilst happiness is always causeless. In the absence of the layer of expectations and demands through which our experience is filtered and negotiated, seeking and resisting are not triggered. We find ourself naturally open to, and one with, the current situation. We are in harmony with the unfolding of the universe.

This oneness with the content of experience is not something that need be practised or manufactured. It is our natural condition prior to the arising of the activity of seeking and resisting. In contrast, the filtering layer of thoughts and feelings through which we navigate our experience needs to be fabricated and maintained.

Happiness is not something that can be found, acquired or caused. It can only be uncovered, revealed and recognised. It is the shining of our own unconditioned being in the midst of experience. We do not need to make an effort to achieve it.

On the contrary, it is the effort of seeking and resisting that veils it. It is for this reason that the sage Ashtavakra said, 'Happiness belongs to that supremely lazy person for whom even blinking is too much trouble'.*

---

* The Ashtavakra Gita.

CHAPTER FOURTEEN

Suffering Is Our Own Activity

*Find the One everywhere and in everything
and there will be an end to pain and suffering.*

ANANDAMAYI MA

The density of the conditioned layer of likes and dislikes that lives in the recesses of our mind, and the frequency with which it is provoked, determines the extent to which seeking and resisting arise within us and veil our innate happiness.

If this filter is relatively transparent, a degree of happiness will percolate into our experience, just as sunlight filters into a room through a fine muslin curtain. If it is opaque and frequently triggered in response to the current situation, our innate peace and happiness will be almost completely obscured, just as a heavy curtain almost entirely blocks out the sun's light. This would equate to the experience of depression.

Most people's experience of suffering fluctuates on a spectrum between these two possibilities, varying only in amplitude and frequency. In the absence of any such filter of likes and dislikes, and the activity of seeking and resisting that accompanies it, the foreground of experience will be pervaded by the happiness that is the nature of its background, just as a room without curtains is filled with light.

In fact, when our bedroom curtains are opened, we do not see the light flowing in through the windows from outside. The light emerges within the room. Likewise, as soon as the layer of likes and dislikes through which we filter and negotiate experience subsides, we are flooded with peace from the inside.

That peace and joy is always there. It is our very nature, simply waiting to be liberated. It is we who close ourself off from it. Happiness is never given or withheld by circumstances. It is solely the outcome of our inner disposition, and we are free at every moment to determine this.

THE STOREHOUSE OF EMOTIONAL RESIDUES

What is it that makes up this layer of likes and dislikes, and what causes it to arise?

The natural condition of awareness is to be open without resistance to all experience, just as physical space offers no resistance to whatever takes place within it. In this case, an experience will arise in awareness, exist for some time and then dissolve back into it, without leaving a trace on it or initiating a process of seeking and resisting.

However, there are some experiences which do not pass unimpeded through awareness but are met with either resistance or the desire to hold on to them. At other times we seek an experience that is not present, which is a form of resistance to our current experience.

Each time we resist an experience that we are facing, hold on to an experience that is passing, or seek an experience that is absent, we are in opposition to our current situation, in defence against what is. As a result, a conflict is generated in our mind.

If this conflict is subsequently resolved, the energy induced by it will dissipate and no trace of it will remain. But if the conflict remains unresolved, it will be stored, not only in the deeper layers of the mind but as a corresponding layer of tension in the body.

The residue of innumerable such unresolved conflicts and tensions lies imprinted in our minds and bodies. Together these constitute the layer of likes and dislikes through which we filter and negotiate experience, and by which our innate happiness is at least partially veiled.

In order to understand how this layer of tendencies and preferences distorts our current experience and influences our response to it, let us return to the analogy of awareness as an open, empty, aware space. All experience arises within this space, and if an experience is neither particularly pleasant nor unpleasant, it will leave no trace in it when it disappears.

However, if any experience is considered especially pleasant or unpleasant and, as a result, we either want to hold on to it or get rid of it, a tension is set up within us. When the experience disappears, a residue of this unresolved tension remains in the space, like a thin layer of cloud, through which the next appearance or experience is filtered.

Although the space of awareness itself is always clear, open and empty, and remains untarnished by any experience, innumerable such emotional residues linger within it and together form the layer of tendencies and preferences.

When we experience anything in life that corresponds to any aspect of the content of this storehouse of emotional residues, the same activity of seeking or resisting will be triggered that caused it to be laid down in the recesses of our mind in the first place. If we find ourself reacting disproportionately to an experience, we can be certain that the residual layer of subliminal feelings has been activated and is making itself known.

For instance, one who was neglected or abandoned as a child may find themselves feeling rejected when their partner looks at another person or even just requires some time on their own. One who was repeatedly undermined as a child may find themselves unreasonably defensive in the face of criticism or regularly reasserting their fragile sense of self through judgement, criticism or argument. They may find themselves easily provoked and prone to taking offence in situations where none was intended.

If these habitual tendencies and residual energies lie below the threshold of the waking-state mind, are we doomed forever to live out their consequences? And if not, is it enough to abide as the presence of awareness in the face of them, or is it necessary to become conscious of them before we are able to get rid of them?

The attempt to get rid of these deep-seated habits and tendencies is itself one such habit. Thus, attempting to get rid of itself is one of the subtler ways that the apparently separate self perpetuates itself.

The apparently separate self thrives on conflict, and if it cannot find another person to oppose, conflict with itself will suffice. So the first step is acceptance, openness. Fortunately, openness is the nature of awareness; it does not have to be manufactured or maintained by effort.

All that is required is to be knowingly the aware openness within which this knot of tension is appearing and with which it is known. Ultimately, the feeling is made of the very awareness within which it appears, just as all waves and currents are made of the ocean.

Organisms that live at the bottom of a well rarely see the light of day and thus remain dormant. However, once a day at midday, the light of the sun shines directly into the shaft of the well and the creatures at the bottom wake up and begin to make their way to the surface.

Similarly, the subliminal layer of thoughts and feelings lies below the threshold of the waking-state mind and is not available to it under normal circumstances. In most cases, these feelings are too painful to face, and so we develop strategies to repress or avoid them.

In this way, their continued existence below the surface of the waking-state mind remains assured, and they continue to exert their subliminal and disruptive influence in our lives. They remain at the bottom of the well, so to speak, often making themselves known in our dreams, or in outbursts of emotional reactivity or destructive behaviour in the waking state. In fact, the more they are ignored or repressed, the more they tend to escalate in intensity as they clamour for our attention.

When we abide as the resistanceless presence of awareness, however, we no longer have a negative or repressive attitude towards such feelings and they are, as a result, allowed to surface. The deep-seated tendencies that lie in the 'unconscious' – the recesses of the mind that are not accessible to the waking state – begin to rise to the surface, attracted by the sun of awareness. This attitude of allowing or welcoming is itself both the exposing and the dissolving of these subliminal tendencies.

As these residual layers of buried emotion dissipate and the natural openness of awareness becomes increasingly obvious, fewer and fewer circumstances in our life retain the power to provoke the activity of seeking and resisting. As a result, we begin to find ourself at peace and fulfilled in circumstances that would have previously been a source of suffering and conflict. We are becoming established in the peace of our true nature.

In the absence of resistance, we no longer separate ourself from the universe as an independently existing entity by disliking what is present or seeking what is not present. In fact, in this case there is no 'we' and the rest of the universe. The universe is a *universe*, not a multiverse. It is a single, indivisible whole.

Our likes and dislikes, and the activity of seeking and resisting which they generate, are the mechanism by which we set ourself up as a separate entity apart from all others and the world. Prior to the arising of that activity, the current situation is a dance of interrelated elements in which no person or thing stands out with its own separate or independent existence.

In the ultimate analysis, there are no people or things. Discrete objects are only such from the perspective of an illusory separate self or ego. Through the activity of seeking and resisting, we artificially extract ourself from the totality of the current situation as an apparently separate and independent entity, the ego.

It is that imaginary entity who, through its own activity of liking and disliking, sets itself apart from all objects and others. As a result, it is always in conflict with the universe, a conflict that it cannot win. Such a one is destined for frustration and disappointment, thereby inflicting suffering upon itself and creating conflict with whomever it comes in contact.

Neither will the activities of such an entity contribute to the long-term good of humanity, although they may make a difference in the short term. The sense of separation that lies at its origin will be imprinted subliminally within all of its activities and will, in time, initiate further conflict. It is for this reason that so many injustices in our civilisation have yet to be remedied in spite of centuries of well-intentioned intervention.

The primary distinction between self and other, which is initiated and perpetuated by the activity of seeking and resisting, is the birth of duality. It is the departure from the Garden of Eden. It is the activity through which the unity of being is fragmented into an apparent multiplicity and diversity of discrete and independently existing objects and selves.

It is the activity of separation, the inevitable consequence of which is unhappiness on the inside, conflict between individuals, communities and nations on the outside, and the exploitation and degradation of the earth.

* * *

Most of the great religious and spiritual traditions contain at their origin the understanding that the peace and fulfilment for which all people long lies in the depths of their own being and is equally available to all people, at all times and under all circumstances, except in rare cases when the safety or well-being of the body is severely compromised.

However, in time this understanding has, to a greater or lesser extent, become mixed with extraneous elements, derived either from the local, temporal customs of the culture in which the tradition originated or from misunderstandings that have mystified and complicated this simple and direct approach.

Devoid of this understanding, our world culture can offer only temporary distraction from uncomfortable feelings through the acquisition of objects, substances, activities, states of mind and relationships. However, as soon as the object, substance, activity, and so on, has worn off or come to an end, the underlying suffering surfaces again, compounding the cycle of suffering, seeking and avoidance that is the basis of all addiction.

I was once on a flight from San Francisco to Seattle, during which I was editing an article on the source of addiction. In an uncanny and poignant moment of synchronicity, the obese woman sitting next to me, with whom I had been conversing off and on during the flight, ordered yet another snack and, turning to me with a sigh of relief which thinly veiled the look of despair in her eyes, said, 'The more I eat, the better I feel'.

Little did she know that the smile I gave her was not only in response to the succinctness with which she had expressed the very syndrome about which I was currently writing but, more importantly, contained a prayer that one day a pause might open up in her cycle of lack, avoidance and fleeting fulfilment, in which the background of peace for which she longed would make itself known to her.

Many people are forever in search of new objects, experiences or relationships in order to mask the unbearable void they feel in the centre of themselves, without realising that what they really seek is to be brought into harmony with the now, irrespective of its content, so as to taste the peace and joy of their true nature.

Each of us is faced with a simple choice at every moment: to embrace our current circumstance and respond to it from that position of openness, or to view the situation through the filter of our past conditioning and reject it on that basis. If we welcome whatever we are currently experiencing – the state of our health, the behaviour of our partner, colleague, parent or child, or the unfolding of events in the world – the same happiness that we would feel on winning the lottery will be released in our current experience.

Imagine the freedom of leading a life in which we know that our happiness is not dependent on anyone or anything. The peace and joy that is the nature of our being would be our constant companion, sometimes present quietly in the background of experience and sometimes overflowing into the foreground.

ERODING THE LAYERS

Almost all psychological suffering is the activity of seeking and resisting that is triggered by our deeply ingrained tendencies. It is, as such, our *own* activity. It is never imposed on us from the outside. If we find ourself blaming someone or something for our unhappiness, it simply indicates that we have not yet clearly understood the mechanism of suffering.

If we think that the loss of our faculties, the behaviour of our partner, the state of our bank balance or the condition of our health is the cause of our unhappiness, we are mistaken. None of these can cause unhappiness unless we give them permission to do so, in which case they will do so. As soon as we withdraw that permission, we immediately take responsibility for our own suffering.

Happiness is the inevitable consequence of facing one's moment-by-moment experience without resistance. Each time we face our current experience with this attitude of openness and surrender, we are, without realising it, undermining and gradually eroding the subliminal store of tendencies and preferences that lies in the depths of our mind.

Likewise, every time we allow our responses and actions to be governed by this subliminal layer, we are strengthening it and setting ourself up for unhappiness in the future.

Shantananda Saraswati used to tell a story about Krishna and his companion on a journey. At the end of the first day's walking, they came to the mansion of a wealthy man and asked if they could rest there for the night. The wealthy man commanded one of his servants to show them to the cattle shed, where they found a place to sleep in the straw. On leaving in the morning, Krishna cast a spell over the man that caused his wealth to double.

The following evening, they came to the house of an impoverished farmer who had only one cow, whose milk he relied on as a source of nourishment and income. They asked the farmer for a place to stay, and in response he cleared out his own modest bedroom for them, shared his meagre evening meal with them, and himself went to sleep in the shed.

The next morning Krishna thanked the farmer and cast a spell on his cow that caused it to become sick and die. After several hours' walking, Krishna's companion could no longer restrain himself and asked him to explain why he had treated their hosts so unfairly.

Krishna replied that the wealthy man had numerous attachments and he had simply doubled them, thereby causing him more misery, while the farmer had only one attachment that stood between him and causeless happiness, and he had simply removed it.

In the context of our exploration, we could liken the two men's attachments to the storehouse of residual energies that remain in our heart long after the event which provoked them has disappeared. Krishna was strengthening the influence of this storehouse in the wealthy man's life. In doing so, he was intensifying the rich man's tendency of seeking and resisting, thus increasing his suffering.

By causing the poor man's cow to die, Krishna was undermining the strength and density of his residual tendencies, purifying his heart of the last vestiges of belief that happiness is dependent on circumstances, thereby enabling him to fully experience that causeless joy.

External circumstances are not responsible for provoking seeking or resisting within us; they are our own responsibility. Instead of reacting emotionally and impulsively, we take a step back from the conditioned layer of likes and dislikes which characterises the separate self or ego and, standing as the presence of awareness, face all experience without resistance.

In the absence or neutralisation of the intermediary layer of likes and dislikes, and the activity of seeking and resisting that is generated by it, the peace and happiness that is the nature of our essential self shines unobstructed in our experience.

It is not the object, substance, activity, state of mind or relationship that we truly seek. All we truly seek is to bring the experience of seeking to an end. We desire only the ending of desire.

'YES' TO ALL EXPERIENCE

The first words I ever heard Francis say were, 'Meditation is a universal "yes" to the totality of one's experience'. Had I fully understood their implication, no further instruction would have been necessary. By simply saying 'yes' to our current situation, irrespective of its content, we are, without necessarily realising it at first, standing in and as our true nature of awareness and opening ourself to its innate qualities of peace and joy.

Just as the empty space of a room unconditionally allows whatever takes place within it without resistance, so our essential nature of pure awareness is open without resistance to all experience. It is thought alone that rises up and says 'no' to the current experience. If that 'no' rises on behalf of the safety or well-being of the body, then it is a direct and legitimate response to the current situation.

Usually, however, the 'no' rises on behalf of an illusory self that we almost constantly try to protect, enhance or fulfil. In fact, the separate self is not an entity in its own right; it is the *feeling* of defence and lack, and the corresponding *activity* of seeking and resisting. To counteract this resistance, one may simply determine to say 'yes' to all experience, unless the safety and well-being of the body are at stake.

This universal welcoming of all experience does not, in fact, need to be practised by the mind. It is the very nature of awareness to allow all experience as it is. In the absence of an intermediary layer of seeking and resisting, we, awareness, are naturally and effortlessly surrendered to or in alignment with our current experience, completely open to it and at the same time free or independent of it.

The moment we separate ourself out from the totality as a separate self or person, we create a state of opposition. The remedy is simple: say 'yes' to experience. In doing so, we align ourself with the universe, moment by moment, rather than pitting ourself against it.

In fact, it is not even necessary to say 'yes' to any experience, for, being inseparable from the universe, we are always and already one with it. There is just the indivisible totality of the situation, and we as an apparent individual are in participation, not conflict, with it, just as a practitioner of Aikido will flow with their opponent's energies rather than resist them.

A friend of mine who used to coach one of the top under-fourteen tennis players in the world told me that whenever she made a mistake or lost a point, she would smile. Instead of provoking in herself 'the failure' – the ego that inhibits the free flow of inspiration in an athlete's game – her smile would erase the error, leaving her open and relaxed to face the next point without any residue of the past to sabotage it.

And I once heard a violinist performing Bach's solo violin partitas in a church. At a critical moment, in the silence between two movements, the mobile phone of a woman sitting in the front row rang with that familiar, persistent ringtone: *da da der der, da da der der, da da der der, der der*. Without a moment's pause, the violinist briefly improvised on the theme before weaving it into the beginning of the next movement. Bach would surely have been delighted!

Actions that are in line with and an expression of the whole tend to restore balance and harmony in situations that have diverged from it. And when the response is over, no separate self rises up to claim authorship. As it says in the Tao Te Ching, such a person 'acts without doing anything'.

Welcoming our current experience is not something that we need *practise*. It is what we *are*. This attitude of welcoming is, as such, the natural condition of our self prior to the arising of the apparently separate self or ego. It is our default state and, therefore, does not have to be maintained by effort. It is for this reason that this approach is said to be an effortless path.

All that is necessary is to cease resisting experience. It is our unimpeded openness to the current experience that enables our innate happiness to be fully felt, irrespective of the content of the experience. In the absence of resistance, our natural state of openness to experience is revealed. Openness is what we are; resistance is what we do.

CHAPTER FIFTEEN

The Way of Surrender

Life could be limitless joy, if we would only
take it for what it is, in the way it is given to us.

TOLSTOY

THE CALL TO RETURN

Just as the transparency of a screen is veiled when a movie begins, so the innate peace and joy that is the nature of our being is obscured when we lose our self in the content of experience. The ensuing suffering is the inevitable consequence of our forgetting or overlooking our essential self.

Suffering is the means by which we are reminded to return from the adventure of experience to our self. In fact, one with a deep interest in truth or reality does not see suffering as something incorrect, wrong or problematic. Rather, they welcome it as a reminder that they have invested their happiness in objective experience, and consider it a loving, if perhaps stringent, invitation to return to their own being.

Everybody experiences this call to recognise their true nature, although not everybody recognises their suffering as such. Indeed, most people respond to the experience of suffering by intensifying their search for peace and happiness in the realm of objective experience, thus further alienating themselves from the peace and joy that lies within them.

Shantananda Saraswati used to tell the story of a disciple, a woman named Kunti, who had one prayer in life: 'Lord, give me some adversity so that I may always remember You'. She instinctively knew that the fulfilment of her personal desires would substantiate the tendency to look for happiness in objective experience rather than finding it, in her language, 'in God's presence in her heart'. Therefore, she prayed to have that temptation removed.

Kunti realised that by having her personal desires fulfilled she was strengthening the ego on whose behalf they arose. By asking for some difficulty, that is, by desiring the curtailment of her desires, she was really praying for the diminishment of her ego, which is another way of saying that she was praying that God's presence might be magnified within her.

Most people's experience is hard enough without their having to ask for further difficulties, but the story of Kunti illustrates the depth of love of truth that is often kindled in the heart of one for whom objective experience has lost, or is beginning to lose, its capacity to be the source of peace and happiness, and the attitude of surrender that accompanies it.

More important than the content of the prayer is the inner attitude of openness from which it arises. Such is the correspondence between our inner lives and the outside world that this attitude of surrender compels the universe to respond.

After all, the universe and the individual are not two separate systems. The individual's desire for happiness is really its desire to be relieved of everything that seems to render it separate from everyone and everything – in other words, its desire to return to the universal.

However, that is said as a concession to the individual's perspective. In reality, the individual is only such from its own partial and, ultimately, illusory perspective. From the perspective of the universal, there is just the universal. The individual is a point of view *of* the universal *within* the universal; it is not an entity in its own right.

What is felt by the individual as its desire for happiness is, in reality, the universe's own impulse to restore the natural order. And because such a desire is impersonal, the universe cannot help but fulfil it. Even if the response is initially only in the form of a book, a meeting with a friend, a video or a chance encounter, if followed with the same pure intention to find happiness or truth, it will sooner or later lead there.

OPEN WITHOUT RESISTANCE

It is also possible that an attitude of surrender may be brought about as a result of our circumstances, without any effort on our own part. In this case, the sheer intensity of the moment will eradicate the filter of thoughts and feelings through which our experience is usually mediated, allowing our innate happiness to shine.

Most experience lies within a range of normality that leaves the habitual, discursive activity of the mind intact, commentating, comparing, analysing, judging, evaluating, responding, and so on. However, at either end of this spectrum there lies a range of experience which is either so pleasant or so unpleasant that the mind is not able to accommodate it within its normal frame of reference. As a result, its activity comes to an end.

Phrases such as, 'It blew my mind', 'I was taken aback', 'It silenced me', 'I was stunned', 'I was blown away' attest to the capacity of certain experiences to bring the mind's activity to an end. In Buddhism the term 'nirvana', used in reference to the cessation of the mind's activity in meditation, literally means 'blown out'. In such moments – timeless moments, for in the absence of mind, there is no time – the mind's essential nature of peace and joy shines forth.

Shortly after I met Francis, in the mid-1990s, we began to host retreats for him at our home in Shropshire. Once a year we would clear out the barns which housed my studio and convert them to a temporary retreat space. On one such occasion, a firing of the kiln was finished the evening before the retreat was due to start. The following morning I woke early to the sound of stones on my bedroom window and the distressed cry of Kofi, my assistant, below. The barns were ablaze.

One of the rafters above the kiln had caught fire, and, the building being some three hundred years old, it did not take long for it to be engulfed in flames. A couple of hours later, Francis's wife Laura called me from Barcelona, where she and Francis were about to board a flight to the UK, in time for the beginning of the retreat that evening.

By that time three fire engines were tackling the blaze and numerous local residents had gathered in the yard between the house and the barns. I described the scene to Laura, and after a brief pause she responded, 'Oh, how interesting! Be aware of the slightest impulse in you to change anything about your current circumstance. See you soon!'

Later that morning, sitting on a low wall in front of the house, watching the now smoking embers of the roof, I felt that I was resting on an ocean of peace. Whether it was in response to Laura's words or simply that the magnitude of the situation was such that it was impossible to resist, I do not know.

Suffice it to say that there was not the slightest resistance in me. Without having made any effort, I simply found myself completely open, without resistance, utterly and spontaneously surrendered to the moment. As a result, the innate peace of my true nature was felt in the background of experience, in spite of the chaos in the foreground. Later I would learn to go there consciously, but for now it felt like a gift.

This attitude of surrender is echoed by Utpaladeva, one of the great sages and poets of the tradition of Kashmir Shaivism, who had a beautiful and simple prayer: 'Due to immersion in You, may I be free of desires for anything but what is; may I be utterly filled with delight, considering every thing and being I see as consisting only of You'.*

As an expression of our true nature, this prayer of supplication becomes, 'I, awareness, knowing the fullness of my own being, am completely free from the desire to change my current experience. I am open without preference and choice to all experience, and thus experience has lost the capacity to deprive me of my innate peace and joy.'

I once knew an elderly man who had lost his three infant sons. He was one of the most open-minded, joyful, warm-hearted people I have ever met. This happened early on in his adult life, and he was faced with a stark choice: to resist the experience, allow his heart to close, and become small-minded, embittered and miserable, or to surrender completely to the experience and allow the pain of it to fully open his heart. His entire life would depend on his choice, and he chose the latter.

He realised that it was not the circumstance itself that had the power to give or deny happiness, but rather his response to it. He simply made the choice to open without resistance to his experience, and as a result, the peace and happiness that lay latent within him was revealed, and indeed overflowed and communicated itself to everyone with whom he came in contact. It was almost impossible to remain closed in his presence, so contagious was his happiness and enthusiasm.

In the absence of this understanding, we will tend to blame the object, situation or person for our suffering. By investing our circumstances with the

---

* Christopher Wallis, *The Recognition Sutras: Illuminating a 1,000-Year-Old Spiritual Masterpiece* (Mattamayura Press, 2017).

power to make us happy or unhappy, we are setting ourself against the entire universe. However, our current circumstances are the result of a chain of innumerable causes that, if we were able to trace them to their origin, would take us back to the Big Bang.

The only other possibility is to embrace our current circumstances, to drop any resistance towards them and to fully align ourself with them. That only need take a moment and is fully within everyone's capacity. It was for this reason that, when Krishnamurti was asked, towards the end of his life, if he had a last secret teaching, he simply replied, 'My secret teaching is this: I don't mind what happens'.

If we invest others with the power to determine our happiness, we will always be negotiating experience in the hopes that it will conform to our idea of how it needs to be in order for us to be happy. Such a life will be one of constant struggle, punctuated by brief moments of relief when circumstances conform to our vision of how they should unfold.

However, as the situation changes, as it inevitably will, these brief moments of respite in which our innate peace and joy is briefly felt will be eclipsed again, and the struggle will resume. It is for this reason that Henry David Thoreau observed that 'The mass of men lead lives of quiet desperation'.*

Even if, at times, circumstances do seem to cooperate with our search for happiness in them, we will, without realising it, be setting ourself up for future misery, for we will be inadvertently strengthening the belief that objective experience is responsible for our happiness. If we surrender our happiness to the vicissitudes of life, it is only a matter of time before the tide will turn.

THE DISSOLUTION OF THE MIND

Traditional cultures formalised the process of surrender by cultivating initiation rites often involving terrifying ordeals or tests of endurance that stretched the capacity of initiates well beyond their normal limits. In response to the ensuing fear of death, they had to access a depth in themselves that childhood had not thus far required, and which heralded the transition to adult life.

*Henry David Thoreau, *Civil Disobedience* (1849).

And what was adult life? A life in which the narrow concerns of the individual were subsumed in, and informed by, the felt understanding of their relationship with the whole. A life in which a person understood and felt that they shared their being with all people, all animals and all things, and acted in a way that was consistent with, and an expression of, this understanding.

In the Zen tradition, a blow from the master's stick was considered an effective, if not rather primitive, means to the same end. A koan, or a question whose purpose is to confound rather than encourage the rational mind, serves the same purpose. In contemplating, for example, the question 'What is but does not exist?', the mind's inability to raise a single thought in response leaves it open and silent, and in that space the light of awareness is revealed.

Indeed, all religious and spiritual traditions have their own repertoire of skilful means whose purpose is to dissolve or expand the boundary of the finite mind and reveal its infinite, impersonal essence.

Recognising that the ego or sense of separation is aggrandised when its object-seeking tendencies are gratified, some of these traditions seek to curtail its activities through discipline, renunciation and asceticism, ranging from moderation and self-restraint to more extreme practices of self-denial.

However, the Tantric traditions recognised desire not only as a means by which the ego or sense of separation may perpetuate and enhance itself but also as a means by which our longing may be returned to its source. In this case, the practitioner may surf a wave of desire all the way back to the shore of awareness, where she will be gently deposited.

Intensely pleasurable experiences can thus be considered to contain within them the same capacity as unpleasant ones to bring the mind's habitual activity to an end, and may, therefore, also be cultivated as spiritual practices.

Leaving aside the fine line between indulgence and transcendence, this tradition recognised that any experience can be a portal to one's true nature, warning only that one should not be seduced by pleasant experiences into stopping short of full and lasting happiness.

As Sri Nisargadatta Maharaj said, 'Increase and widen your desires until nothing but reality can fulfil them'.* That is, do not be satisfied with fleeting

*Sri Nisargadatta Maharaj, *I Am That* (Acorn Press, 2012 rev.).

moments or periods of happiness. Seek nothing less than lasting happiness, and understand that lasting happiness can only be found in that which lasts.

SURRENDERING THE ILLUSORY SELF

Sometimes I feel as if everything in my life has been encouraging me to make this investigation into the nature of myself, but at the same time I'm afraid of it. It's a threat not only to my identity but to my way of life.

For most people, their interest in these matters, and their willingness to explore their experience in this way, is initiated by reading a book, watching a video, hearing a talk or having a conversation with a friend. However, it may also happen that one's circumstances conspire to initiate this process without any interest on their part. In this case, the sudden loss of one's customary identity, even if only temporarily, may be accompanied by great fear.

In extreme cases, it may feel like dying. Indeed, it is a kind of death! But it is not the death of our self; it is the dissolution of an illusory self: an image, an idea, a feeling. It is the disentanglement of our self from the elements of experience with which we previously identified: thoughts, memories, history, activities, relationships, and so on.

In the absence of the familiar objects and experiences with which we normally identify ourself, this unsolicited plunge into our true nature may also be disorientating and we may shrink from it, preferring our old identity in spite of the suffering that inevitably accompanies it.

However, such an experience is like a crack in our familiar sense of ourself. We may plaster it over, through fear of the unknown, with strategies that once worked well for us, but we will never be the same again, nor will the strategies be as effective as they once were, or at least seemed to be.

In quiet moments, when the mind is open and unfocused, we may be disturbed by the memory of an unknown but strangely familiar presence within, inviting us in an unknown direction to which we still seem to have no access.

It is also possible that the outer form of our life, which may have served us well thus far, begins to fall apart, without any corresponding intuition or revelation of our true nature. The old has broken down but the new has not yet emerged. In the absence of the correct interpretation, we may feel hopeless.

Previously we would have shrunk from the uncertainty of this new possibility on the brink of which we stand, and reached for the known, the familiar, the secure. However, in this case the known has lost its credibility. There is no way forward: the future is an abyss and the present unbearable. For some of us this crisis will initiate the return journey into the depths of our being; for others it may lead to a life of resignation, hopelessness or despair.

Once, while attending a retreat with Francis and staying with him and Laura at their home in southern California, I had a dream. It was the night before the final day of the retreat, and in the dream, it was also the last day of a retreat with Francis, but in a different house. It was a large house with many rooms, and I was looking everywhere for Francis to say goodbye to him.

Eventually I came upon a small room, dark because it had no windows, in the centre of the house. As I entered from a door in one corner of the room, Francis entered through a door in the opposite corner. We met in the middle and embraced. I rubbed his back with one of my hands – a gesture he would often make when saying goodbye to me – and said, 'Thank you, thank you, thank you!'

I was standing on tiptoes and, feeling a little unstable, reached out behind me for a rail to steady myself. At that moment, a voice inside said clearly, 'Don't hold on to anything you know'. I let go of the rail and our two bodies dissolved into one another. When our bodies re-emerged, he said to me, 'When speaking to people, remember to tell them who it is that bears the light'.

So you can give yourself entirely to this understanding. It is not necessary to worry about the effect it will have on your life. All you will lose is your unhappiness on the inside and your conflicts on the outside. As you no longer separate yourself from everyone and everything, you will most likely find that the universe begins to cooperate with you rather than seeming to frustrate you.

You will find yourself leading a creative, productive life, without feeling that you did anything particular to bring it about. In fact, you didn't! You simply ceased separating yourself from the rest of the universe and thus allowed the universe to fulfil its purpose though you.

CHAPTER SIXTEEN

Take Refuge in the Now

The Master arrives without leaving,
sees the light without looking,
achieves without doing a thing.

LAO TZU

THE ADDICTION TO THINKING

Resistance to our current experience varies in degree from a mild sense of boredom, expectation or lack, which barely registers on the scale of suffering, to intense aversion. In most cases, our suffering takes place on a scale between these two possibilities.

However, irrespective of the intensity of our suffering, we are in almost all cases motivated to avoid it through the acquisition of objects, substances, activities, circumstances or relationships. Our avoidance, in turn, varies in intensity from addiction to substances and activities at one end of the spectrum to the comparatively benign activity of compulsive thinking at the other. In each case, the purpose of the activity is solely to distract us from the discomfort of our current experience.

Drugs, tobacco, alcohol, excessive eating and over-working are some of the most common means that suffice for this purpose. Even spiritual practice can be appropriated by the separate self or ego to perpetuate the activity of seeking and resisting which characterise its illusory identity. However, by far the most ubiquitous means of avoidance is compulsive thinking.

Many of the more obvious and extreme means by which we avoid the discomfort of our current experience are bad for our health and, in some cases, illegal. However, excessive thinking is neither bad for our health, at least not overtly so, nor illegal, and is thus the default avenue of escape for most people.

Indeed, thinking seems so innocuous that most people are not even aware that it is one of the main ways we avoid the sense of lack. For this reason, it has escaped diagnosis as one of the most successful ways we subtly perpetuate it. However, when we are determined to find the real cause of our suffering, we become increasingly sensitive to the more or less subtle means by which we escape it.

There are, of course, many legitimate reasons for thinking – a response to the current situation, planning for the future, evaluating the past, scientific endeavour, investigative or celebratory purposes, and creativity are amongst them – but most thinking serves none of these. Its purpose is simply to take us away from the discomfort of our current experience.

If we take any train of thought and ask of it, 'Where are you going and why?' the response will often be, 'I am venturing into the past or future in order to avoid having to face the discomfort of my present circumstance'.

In this way, most people believe that in order to find the peace and happiness for which they long they must reject their current experience, which is deemed insufficient, and venture into the past or future, which seem to hold the promise of fulfilment. Ironically, our suffering *begins* the moment we escape from our current experience into an imagined future or a remembered past.

In fact, if we want relief from our suffering, all that is required is to return from our happiness-seeking adventure in the past and future and come back to our current experience. We must return to the now. Where previously we sought to escape from our present suffering into a future which we believed held the promise of happiness, instead we take refuge in the now, the only place suffering cannot stand. In this way we find, at the very heart of our experience, the happiness we previously sought by avoiding it.

Many of our thoughts arise for the purpose of controlling the events of our life so that they will produce exactly the conditions that we believe are required for us to experience lasting peace and joy.

However, our current circumstances are the growing edge of millions of years of evolution. For instance, the behaviour of a friend, partner or colleague is the product of centuries of conditioning. What are the chances that these circumstances are going to coincide with our personal expectations and demands?

The only reason we are not at peace and filled with joy now is that circumstances do not conform to our idea of how they should be. One who understands this aligns what they want with what they have, rather than trying to conform what they have to what they want.

Suffering is never imposed on us; it is our own activity of seeking and resisting. Happiness can never be acquired by us; it is our own nature.

THERE ARE NO PROBLEMS

Circumstances never announce themselves as problematic. They simply present themselves. From the perspective of awareness, there are situations; for the ego, there are problems. It is our resistance that turns a situation into a problem, that turns our innate peace into suffering. And it is the withdrawal of this resistance that reveals the underlying peace. For the ego there is suffering; for awareness there is peace.

Awareness does not negotiate experience. Its nature is simply to welcome whatever arises, allow whatever exists and let go of whatever vanishes.

And just as space is never harmed or destroyed by anything that takes place within it, so we, awareness, are never hurt or overwhelmed by anything that takes place in experience. We, awareness, are open to all experience, allowing all experience without resistance, defenceless and yet indestructible.

This openness without resistance to all experience is not something we, as a person, need *practise*, because it is our *nature*, just as the empty space of a room does not need to practise allowing whatever appears within it. Openness without resistance is what we are, not what we do.

Resistance to what is appears in the form of a single thought: 'I don't want what is present; I want what is not present'. All suffering is caused by that thought alone. As soon as that thought rises up in between our self and our experience of the world, our innate happiness is veiled and suffering ensues.

In the absence of any resistance to experience, the peace and happiness that is our very nature simply shines by itself. This openness without resistance to all experience is not a *state* of the mind. It is the natural condition of the mind in the absence of seeking and resisting. Happiness is the *nature* of the mind; suffering is a *state* of the mind.

It is only the extent to which we open ourself unreservedly and unconditionally to any experience that governs our happiness. Our true nature of peace and joy is always present within our own being; it *is* our own being.

It is our own resistance to experience, in the form of thinking and feeling, that closes us off from the ever-present background of our innate joy, just as clouds obscure the blue sky.

What is it that causes this opening of the cloud cover? What is it that gives us access to this ever-present background of happiness? Simply our openness without resistance to the current situation.

Every moment of happiness is a window in our experience onto the ever-present background of our essential being, whose nature is happiness itself.

The only reason it is not fully felt by everyone all the time is the single thought that dictates that circumstances should be other than they are right now, that they should conform to our preconceived idea of them.

We have allowed a single thought to steal our happiness. It is that thought alone that stands between each of us and the innate peace and joy that lives in our hearts, or rather that *is* the very heart of us. We are free at every moment to choose happiness in spite of circumstances, not because of them.

The nature of our being is peace and joy itself. All that is necessary in order to access our self and, as a result, its innate peace and joy, is to come back to our own being again and again, and to stand as that in the face of all experience.

When we become accustomed to knowing and feeling ourself as the presence of awareness, problems cease. Or rather, our *resistance* to problems ceases and, as a result, the so-called problem itself is no longer experienced as such. It is experienced as simply a situation to be faced with openness and equanimity, thereby giving it the best possible chance of a harmonious resolution for all parties involved.

Situations that were once met with resistance or emotional reactivity are now welcomed as an opportunity to understand the extent to which we have invested our happiness in objective experience. Instead of frustrating our search for happiness in the world, such situations cooperate with the revelation of the peace and happiness that is the very nature of our being.

* * *

There are some situations that I find so hurtful that I cannot stay open to them or to the person involved. Should I just accept such situations?

It is important to recognise whether our response to such a situation arises on behalf of truth, love and justice or on behalf of a hurt self. If the latter, then it is legitimate to take whatever action may be appropriate to bring intelligence and love to bear on the situation. However, every time we react emotionally to a person or situation, we betray the fact that our happiness is invested in them. In doing so, we are, without at first realising it, strengthening the power that objective experience has over us, thereby alienating ourself from our innate peace and joy.

Even if our reaction were to bring about the desired result in the short term, we would have strengthened the underlying feeling from which it came, and ultimately the separate self or ego on whose behalf that feeling arose, thus perpetuating the tendency to react in the same way to a similar situation in future.

Unaware that our suffering is entirely our own activity, we will project its cause onto the person or situation. It is for this reason that, in spite of our efforts, we find ourself facing the same problematic situations over and over again in life. It is not the situation itself that is problematic; it is our response to it that is as such. Ultimately there are no problems; there are just situations.

However, until this is clear, apparently problematic situations will continue to occur in our life, provoking and testing us until we have understood their message, namely, that we should withdraw from people and circumstances the expectation or demand that they be a source of happiness.

When this has been understood, we cease using the world for the sake of our happiness and start using our happiness for the sake of the world. And just as the world previously appeared to us in the form of circumstances that mirrored our inner state of resistance, so now the world will realign itself with our new attitude of openness.

In fact, the world has not changed. The filter of seeking and resisting through which we previously perceived the world and negotiated our response to it has simply become more transparent, and as a result, the world appears in a new light.

BECOMING ESTABLISHED IN AND AS OUR TRUE NATURE

Ever since I first became aware of awareness in the background of my experience, I seem to travel back and forth between it and my thoughts and feelings in the foreground. This gives me moments of respite from the suffering that I used to experience almost continually, but I long for lasting peace.

Imagine a woman who lives in a small apartment on a noisy street in the city and commutes to and from work every day on public transport. After a busy and exhausting week, she drives a couple of hours into the countryside, where she has a small cottage, and enjoys a peaceful, relaxing weekend. On Sunday night she returns to the city and the cycle is repeated, week in, week out, back and forth from her stressful life in her apartment to the peace and quiet of her cottage.

One day she has simply had enough: she requests permission from her employer to work from home, sells her apartment and moves into her cottage. Her life ceases to oscillate from the stress and anxiety of life in the city to the peace and quiet of life in the country. She continues to work, and is as productive as ever, but without leaving the peace of her home.

In the same way, we seem for a while to travel back and forth between the turbulence of our thoughts, feelings, sensations and perceptions in the foreground of experience, and the inherently peaceful and unconditionally fulfilled presence of awareness in the background.

However, in time, our true nature of awareness will cease being something that we seem to *visit* from time to time and will be understood and felt simply to be what we *are*. To be knowingly the presence of awareness will become our natural condition, and no effort will be required either to return there or to maintain it. It will become our new identity. We move in. We live there, as that.

The only reason why resting in and as our being may initially require some effort is due to the previously unnoticed habit of almost continuously and exclusively losing our self in, and identifying our self with, objective experience. It is only the initial attempt we make to counteract that habit that seems to require an effort.

To illustrate this, take the example of a closed fist. The natural condition of the hand is open and relaxed. However, a hand which has been clenched for some time will become accustomed to this new position which, if maintained, will seem to become its new norm. In order to return the hand to its natural position of openness and relaxation, an effort will initially be required.

Once the hand has been open for some time, no effort will be required to maintain it; it has simply returned to its natural position. In fact, the effort to open the hand was not really a *new* effort. It was simply the relaxation of a *previous* effort which had become so habitual that it was no longer noticed as such.

The return to our true nature of peace and happiness proceeds in a similar way. What may at first seem to be an effort to disentangle our self from the content of experience is, in fact, the relaxation of a previous effort of which we were unaware. It only seems to be an effort because we had become so habituated to an almost constant state of more or less subtle seeking and resisting.

In time, as we become accustomed to resting in or as being, less and less effort will be required, because the habit of losing our self in, or identifying our self with, the objective content of experience will have become weakened by practice, just as a rocket requires less energy to navigate space once it has escaped the gravitational pull of the earth.

At some point, resting as being is felt and understood to be our natural condition. As we abide more and more in our self, our deep-seated tendencies gradually come to the surface and are dissolved. The almost constant state of dissatisfaction that seemed to have accompanied us most of our life simply leaves us, without our necessarily even noticing.

At this point, no further practice is required. The practice of returning again and again to our essential being turns into the love of simply being. And in that love of simply being, the peace and joy which is our nature shines forth.

Attending to Painful Emotions

In the depths of winter, I finally learned
that within me there lay an invincible summer.

ALBERT CAMUS

THREE WAYS TO ATTEND TO PAINFUL EMOTIONS

From the non-dual perspective, what is the best way to deal with really intense,
painful emotions?

The impulse to avoid the dissatisfaction of our current experience can be followed in one of three directions: one, outwards towards an object, substance,
activity or relationship in an attempt to escape the discomfort of it; two,
inwards to the self on whose behalf the sense of lack arises; or three, towards
the feeling of lack or dissatisfaction itself.

The first approach could be called the way of avoidance and is the default
approach for most people. The second could be called the way of self-enquiry
or investigation, and the third, the way of openness.

In the way of avoidance, the intense, painful emotion is considered unbearable and we distract ourself from it with objects, substances, activities
and relationships. In this case the sense of lack, and the separate self or ego
on whose behalf it arises, will remain intact, albeit temporarily masked by
the distraction. However, as soon as the object, substance, activity or relationship has passed or changed, the underlying sense of lack will resurface.

In an attempt to avoid it, we may again turn away from it towards the
distraction of our choice, only this time a slightly stronger dose will be
required. In this way a perpetual cycle of lack, avoidance, temporary fulfilment
and inevitable failure will lead eventually to despair and, often, addiction.

To illustrate the difference between the second and third approaches –
the way of enquiry or investigation and the way of openness – imagine

a professional boxing match. When the two boxers are at a distance of about one metre from one another, they are dangerous and in danger. In the interval between rounds, each goes to his respective corner, where he is safe. However, during the fight itself it is not possible for either boxer to retire to his corner. So what does a boxer do if he wants respite from the intensity of the fight? He comes close to his opponent and wraps his arms around him in a 'clinch', thereby neutralising him. He finds safety in closeness.

The path of self-enquiry is the equivalent of the break that the boxers take between rounds. That is, in self-enquiry we *increase* the apparent distance between our self and our suffering. We disengage from the struggle with our emotions, trace our way back through the layers of our experience, and come to rest in and as the presence of awareness.

In reality, awareness is so utterly, intimately one with all experience that it cannot separate itself from any experience and stand at a distance from it, any more than a screen can be separated from an image. At the same time, awareness is utterly free and independent from the content of experience. So the analogy of the boxers retiring to their respective corners is simply meant to illustrate this disentanglement from the content of experience and the return to the peace of our true nature.

In other words, in the way of enquiry or investigation, we turn away from the feeling and investigate the suffering self: Who is this 'I' on whose behalf my suffering arises? The way of self-enquiry is, as such, an inward-facing path, in which we turn away from the unpleasant emotion and question the 'I' at its heart, thereby tracing our way back to our essential, irreducible being, the presence of awareness. It is often initiated, at least in the early stages, by a process of negation or discrimination, in which we discard every aspect of our experience that is not essential to us: 'I am not this, not this, not this'. In the Western tradition it is known as the Via Negativa.

In the way of openness, we turn *towards* the unpleasant emotion and embrace it. This is like the clinch during the boxing match. We *decrease* the distance between our self and our suffering. We turn *towards* it. We embrace the danger, neutralising it in our welcoming presence.

In fact, we need not turn towards any afflictive emotion; it would be enough to cease turning away from it. The presence of awareness that we essentially are is already turned towards, or open without resistance to, all experience. This openness is what we are, not what we do. It does not need to be practised.

However, all psychological suffering arises because we have temporarily forgotten or overlooked that we are this resistanceless presence of awareness and, as a result, have mistaken our self for a separate self or ego. Therefore, it is legitimate to suggest to this apparently separate self or ego that it turn towards the suffering that it would normally seek to avoid.

Some courage may initially be needed as we face the discomfort of the sense of lack from which we have been in flight for much of our lives. However, by facing the sense of lack in this way we will be withholding from it the one thing that it requires for its survival, namely, our resistance to it.

By welcoming what was previously unacceptable to us we are, without necessarily realising it at first, taking our stand as the presence of awareness, and it is only a matter of time before the peace and joy that is its very nature will begin to emerge and percolate into the foreground of experience.

In the way of openness, we go deeply into the emotion itself and find at its very core the peace we previously sought by avoiding it. It is a path in which we turn *towards* the content of experience. It is the way of surrender, of embrace, the way of 'yes', the Via Positiva.

To summarise the distinction between these two approaches, when we say, 'I feel lonely', there are two elements to the experience: I, myself, and the feeling of loneliness. In the way of self-enquiry or investigation, we explore the 'I' and ignore the loneliness; in the way of openness, we embrace the loneliness and ignore the 'I'.

It is legitimate to explore either of these approaches. Both pathways, if followed all the way, lead to the same conclusion, namely, the dissolution of the sense of separation and the suffering that inevitably attends it, and the return to the peace and happiness that is our natural condition.

INVESTIGATING THE 'I'

I understand this approach in theory, but can you give an example of what the way of investigation looks like in practice?

Imagine someone were to say to you, 'Isn't it a beautiful day today?' Would you be upset by it?

No.

You hear the words, you register their meaning and they vanish without leaving any trace in you, and without your wanting either to hold on to them because they are so pleasant or to get rid of them because they are so unpleasant. But imagine that someone were to say something that you find hurtful. In this case, the words don't just pass through you without leaving a trace. Something in you resists the words and, as a result, you feel upset. Who is it that is upset?

I am upset.

Tell us about the 'I' that is upset.

My image or idea of myself. Usually I would feel like, 'They shouldn't have done that'.

Can an image or an idea be upset?

No.

So who or what is it that is upset? You refer to whatever that is as 'I'. '*I* am upset by what he said.' '*I* am hurt by her behaviour.' Who or what is this upset 'I'? This is how to look for the 'I'. When you hear the words 'Isn't it a beautiful day today?' there is no holding on to or resisting the words. No 'I' rises up to say, 'I like it' or 'I don't like it'. The words just float unimpeded through awareness and leave no trace on it. What is it that rises up and says, '*I* am upset'? Is the awareness that heard the supposedly hurtful words upset?

No.

Awareness is like an open, empty, knowing, space-like presence; it cannot be hurt, stained, tarnished, moved, changed or destroyed by words, or indeed by anything else, any more than empty space can be hurt or destroyed by whatever takes place within it.

Imagine throwing a ball through empty space. The ball just flows through the space until it meets with some resistance: someone raises a hand or it hits the wall. In the absence of any such resistance, the ball just flows through the space. Likewise, without the rising of the 'I' that says, 'I like it, I want it' or 'I dislike it, I don't want it', the words will flow through you without affecting you in any way.

Now, when you hear the supposedly hurtful words, something rises up and resists the words and says, 'I don't like it'. The counterpart of the thought 'I don't like it' is felt in the body as an emotion of hurt or suffering. What is this 'I' that rises up and resists the words? On whose behalf does the resistance arise? It is obviously not the 'I' of awareness.

The 'I' that I think I am.

Go to that 'I'. Try to find it. What exactly is it? Where is it? What is it made of? Your hurt feeling is arising on its behalf, so you must know it. In fact, most of your life revolves around it. What do you find when you go towards it?

I guess it's a story.

Don't guess. It is only necessary to guess about something you don't know. But you know yourself more intimately than you know any other thing. Your whole life revolves around 'I'. Be specific. What is that? It's a story, yes, but can a story be upset?

No.

On whose behalf is the story being told? Who is the protagonist of the story?

Well, me.

You point to your body when you say 'me', but is your body upset by these words?

It feels upset. I get tightness in my stomach and chest.

Is there anything to the tightness in your stomach or chest other than a mild sensation?

No.

Can a sensation be upset?

No.

The tightness in your chest and stomach is the *result* of being upset; it is the echo of the upset in your body, but it is not the upset itself, nor is it the upset self. Your cheek or nose or shoulder doesn't get upset when you hear the words. So look again for the 'I' that is hurt or upset. What do you find?

I don't find a thing. I just find…I guess just what I identify as me, that somehow I've been wronged.

Okay, but who or what is that 'I' that has been wronged? It is not your body, a thought or an image that has been wronged, nor is it awareness itself.

So it's some sense of myself.

What is that?

I don't know what it is.

It would be as well to find out. Unless and until you find a self other than the self of awareness, don't presume there is one, and, above all, don't spend the rest of your life thinking, feeling, acting and relating on its behalf.

When I look for myself, I find thoughts, feelings and sensations, but I don't find an actual self or entity.

Yes, and what is going to happen to your upset, your suffering, when you discover that the separate self on whose behalf it has arisen is not there?

I assume it would just go away.

Yes, the upset or the suffering dissipates because there is no separate, independently existing entity or self present either to be upset or not to be upset. When it is seen clearly that there is no personal self, the issue of getting upset just doesn't arise.

Now, what is it that gives you the undeniable sense of being your self? Where does your basic sense of identity come from?

Just from awareness.

Yes! Tell us about that.

(Long silence)

I like your response! Try to say something true about your self, awareness, even if it requires some concession to the limits of language.

It...it just is. I just am. And I am aware.

Yes, you, awareness, are present and aware. Anything else?

(Long silence)

Can you be disturbed?

No, I am always in peace.

Do you lack anything?

No, the question itself seems ridiculous!

Yes! And what is the common name for the absence of lack?

Happiness!

Exactly, happiness is your nature. You do not need to go anywhere or do anything to find it. It is always available within yourself, as your self.

Your investigation into the nature of your self has taken you from the happiness you seek to the happiness you are. That is self-enquiry in practice.

EMBRACING OUR SUFFERING

Can you say more about the way of openness in our actual experience, and how it differs from self-enquiry?

Just as it is only possible for the eye to see something that is at a distance from itself, so it is only possible to know and, therefore, name something as an object of experience when we stand apart from it as a separate subject of experience.

Awareness cannot stand apart from any experience and know it from a distance. It is so utterly, intimately one with experience that it cannot label it, let alone consider it good or bad, right or wrong, pleasant or unpleasant. It is knowledge through intimacy, as opposed to knowledge through conception and abstraction.

It is the apparently separate self or ego that detaches itself from experience and views it from a distance. It is only from this apparent distance that we are able to feel and label our experience as fear, anxiety, shame, sorrow, and so on, and thus deem it unpleasant. All our suffering exists in the illusory space between the subject and the object of experience, just as the danger exists in the space between the two boxers when they are one metre apart.

In the way of self-enquiry, we *increase* that distance, in the sense that we explore the 'I' and disregard the emotion. In the way of openness, we do the opposite: we collapse the apparent distance between our self and the afflictive emotion, such as fear, anxiety, shame, guilt or sorrow. We turn towards the experience from which we would normally turn away. We welcome that which we would normally reject. We find sanctuary by embracing our suffering.

This attitude is illustrated in the Grimm Brothers' fairy story *The Frog Prince*, in which a frog offers to retrieve a princess's golden ball from the lake in which she has lost it, in return for her friendship. After she agrees to the deal, the frog retrieves the ball, but the princess forgets her side of the bargain.

However, later that evening, while the princess is having dinner with her father, the king, the frog returns to the royal palace to remind her. Reluctantly she invites him inside and allows him to eat from her plate. Later that night, upon his further insistence, the princess allows the frog to sleep on her pillow, and finally she embraces it.

The next morning the princess wakes to find a handsome prince in bed next to her! When the princess embraced that which was most distasteful to her, it turned into that for which she longed above all else.

In the way of openness, we understand and feel our self as the open, empty, resistanceless presence of awareness, and we turn towards any afflictive emotion from which we would normally turn away. We allow the frog into the palace, albeit somewhat reluctantly!

This may evoke some initial resistance in us, and therefore some courage may be required not to escape from it into thinking, activities, objects and so on. When this first wave of resistance subsides in our allowing presence, we invite the experience closer. We do not simply tolerate or allow it; we positively welcome it. The frog is eating from our plate!

Again, we may pause, allowing the habitual and familiar tendency to turn away from uncomfortable feelings, first to be exposed and then neutralised in our welcoming. Our resistance is diminishing, and with it the afflictive quality of the emotion. The frog is sleeping on our pillow!

Finally, we bring the feeling so close that we can no longer separate ourself from it and label it fear, anxiety, shame, guilt, sorrow, and so on, let alone consider it unpleasant. The subject and the object – the feeler and the felt, the knower and the known – have merged. In the absence of a separate feeler or knower – the apparently separate subject of experience from whose perspective the feeling is labelled and resisted – there is just the raw experience itself, pure feeling. It is neither good nor bad, right nor wrong, pleasant nor unpleasant.

We know when we have reached this stage when we can genuinely say to the feeling, 'You are welcome inside me forever'. At that point, our suffering, that is, our resistance to experience, has come to an end, not because we have successfully found a way to avoid it but because we have had the courage to fully turn towards and embrace it. We have taken the experience so deeply into our self that it has dissolved in our openness.

We have, as they say in the tradition of Kashmir Shaivism, devoured our emotion. We have kissed the frog! In this way we find, at the very heart of our most painful feelings, the happiness we previously sought by turning away from them. The frog has turned into a handsome prince.

*　*　*

Most of the time my suffering is simply too intense to face and I find myself doing anything I can to avoid it. I'm currently dealing with the end of a relationship and the fact that my ex-partner is already in a new relationship only four days after we split up. I'm just stuck in that suffering. Can you give me one thing to do?

Close your eyes and, referring only to your direct, immediate experience, that is, without referring to thought or memory, tell us about your current experience.

Well, I'm just sitting here.

Without reference to thought or memory, how do you know you are sitting here? If your eyes are closed, all there is to the experience of sitting is the current sensation. Tell us about that sensation without adding any interpretation from your past.

It's a sensation of my body sitting on a chair.

With your eyes closed and without reference to thought or memory, how do you know that the current sensation is a sensation 'of a body', let alone 'sitting on a chair'? 'Body', 'sitting' and 'chair' are concepts, based on memory, that are overlaid onto the raw, unnameable sensation itself. They are the subtitles on the movie, not the movie itself. In fact, even to label it a sensation is too much. There is just a vibration of a certain intensity appearing in the field of experience. Tell us about that vibration.

It's...(long pause)...I can't say anything about it.

Do you like it or dislike it?

It is neither pleasant nor unpleasant. It just is what it is.

Now take the image of your ex-boyfriend with his new partner, but don't refer to any thoughts about the image. Just experience the raw image without commentary. Tell us about it.

It's…(long pause)…again, I can't say anything about it.

Do you like it or dislike it?

Again, it just is what it is. Anything I feel or say about it would be added to the raw experience.

Perfect! Is there any suffering present in your current experience?

No!

What is the common name for this absence of suffering?

Peace or happiness.

Where did you go to find this peace and happiness?

I didn't go anywhere.

Exactly! You didn't escape from your current experience.

No, actually, I stayed with my current experience!

That is the great secret! People normally believe that their suffering takes place now and that relief from suffering is to be found in the future or past. However, our suffering begins the moment we try to escape from our current experience into an imagined future or a remembered past. If you want relief from your suffering – that is, if you want peace and happiness – simply stay with your current experience.

There is a practice in the Theravada Buddhist text the Satipatthana Sutta in which students are asked to focus on a 'bloated, livid and festering' corpse.* The student is asked to sit with the experience for as long as it takes for their repulsion to be neutralised in their disinterested contemplation.

---

*As translated from the Pali by Thanissaro Bhikkhu (2008).

Visualising my ex making love with his partner is much worse than imagining a rotting corpse!

Well, you are a mature student! However, a mature student is not necessarily one who has been on the path for a long time, but rather one who has the courage, the love and the clarity to go for the truth of their experience irrespective of the cost to their personal life.

But I forget that it's here when I'm so stuck in my feelings.

Keep reminding yourself until it becomes natural to simply live in the now. Most people live in the past or future and only visit the now briefly on the fulfilment of a desire, in the pause between thoughts or in the peace of deep sleep. Make the now your home and only visit the past or the future when required to do so for practical, celebratory or investigative purposes. Everything you have ever truly longed for lives there.

But I can't stop my thoughts about my past relationship.

It is only possible to entertain one thought at a time. The whole weight of your suffering is contained in a single thought. Cease investing that thought with the power to make you miserable. At any moment of suffering, just ask yourself the question, 'Without reference to thought or memory, where is my suffering?' All suffering is contained in the imaginary space between what I have and what I want. Make what you have what you want and there will be no room for suffering.

There's a part of me that feels that I need to be doing a little suffering.

That is your freedom! But why do you feel you need to suffer?

I think it's partly because I've created this story: I'm a woman whose relationship has ended. All my friends and family are in this with me, like, 'Oh, you poor thing, this is really terrible.'

Yes, the suffering is in the story, not the situation itself. Who is telling you that story?

I am telling it to myself!

Yes, simply stop telling yourself that story.

It's kind of added to by the people around me. I think it's society as well that does that.

Don't blame others for your suffering. No person or situation imposes suffering on you. Your suffering is your own activity. All suffering is resistance, and all resistance is contained in the thought 'I don't like what is present; I want what is not present'. Have the courage and the clarity to see that.

It feels quite hard. There's a justified part of me that wants to say, 'Well, no, what he did was wrong and unkind'. I hear what you're saying, but there's that going on as well. Even when I just talk to people, they're like, 'Oh my God, that must be really awful'.

Choose carefully whom you speak to. Seek truth, not consolation. It is truth alone that will liberate you. Have the courage and the clarity to face your experience without turning away from it. The heavy burden of suffering that you have been carrying around with you, not just this last week but all your life, is contained in a single thought. Can you taste the peace and freedom that is available to you if you don't refer to that single thought?

Yes.

You are like someone in prison with the door wide open. Just walk through it.

I think I'm just a professional sufferer.

Retire!

Yes, I look forward to retiring.

Don't look forward to it! Hand in your notice and leave! You are already free.

CHAPTER EIGHTEEN

The Unity of Being

The Kingdom of God is within you and it is outside of you.

JESUS

If we were to distil the contents of this book thus far into a single phrase, it might read, 'The awareness of being is happiness'. This understanding summarises the first universal truth that is the source of all the great religious, spiritual and philosophical traditions and which, when clearly seen, brings the search for happiness to an end.

However, we may object on two grounds: one, that we arrived at this understanding by making a distinction between awareness and the content of experience, thereby maintaining an inherent dualism; and two, that this understanding takes care of the individual but neglects society and the environment at large.

As we have seen, most of us are so exclusively identified with our thoughts, feelings and sensations that we have allowed ourselves to be defined by them. Our being seems to be coloured by experience. Therefore, in order to recognise our essential nature, it is first necessary to divest our being of the qualities and limitations it seems to have acquired from experience.

This involves turning within, sinking into being to the exclusion of objective experience. In this process, being is initially revealed as the neutral ground that underlies all experience, and then this neutrality gives way to peace and, in time, joy. As Yvan Amar, a Dutch teacher of non-duality once said, 'Peace is happiness at rest; happiness is peace in motion'.

However, this is not a static process. In the words of Rumi, beautifully rendered by Coleman Barks, the investigation into the essential nature of our self is to 'Flow down and down in always widening rings of being'.*

---

*Jelaluddin Rumi, 'A Community of the Spirit', *Selected Poems*, translated by Coleman Barks (Penguin Classics, 2004).

As we sink more and more deeply into being, or, stated from the perspective of being, as being is progressively divested of the qualities it seems to have acquired from experience, it grows 'wider'; it loses its limitations. Our being is not *our* being. There is no 'our', no 'me' to whom being belongs. There is just utterly intimate yet impersonal, infinite being.

Gradually, or occasionally suddenly, the mists of belief that have shrouded our being evaporate. Being loses its apparent limitations and is understood to extend beyond the individual. It is shared, universal, whole.

Being shines in each of us as the am-ness of our self and in the world as the is-ness of all things. This utterly intimate and yet impersonal, infinite being that was first recognised within us as the experience of peace and happiness is now revealed as the being from which everyone and everything derives its apparently independent existence. This is the second aspect of the non-dual understanding: we share our being with everyone and everything.

LOSING THE SENSE OF SEPARATION

When I was seven years old, apparently I said to my mother that I thought everything was God's dream. I cannot help but notice that now, more than fifty years later, I have not evolved very much, although I express myself in rather more sophisticated terms!

Later on, in my teenage years, I developed a great admiration for the Romantic poets, with their reverence for the all-pervasive spirit which permeated the natural world and, at the same time, lay in the depths of their own heart. In particular, I noticed how their use of words had the ability to induce in myself the same experience from which their poetry originated. My love of the beauty and power of language perhaps comes from this period.

Around that time, I also developed a love of being in nature. Walking in the landscape, I would often notice that my mind would spontaneously quieten and, at the same time, I would lose the sense of being enclosed within the body. The landscape felt as intimate as my body, and my body became as open and expansive as the landscape.

I felt that I was melting into a presence that was familiar and yet, at the same time, much larger than anything I knew of myself. A presence 'whose dwelling is the light of setting suns, and the round ocean, and the living air, and the blue sky, and in the mind of man'.*

Many years later, after meeting Francis, I was astonished to find that this expansion of the body into the surrounding space, and the corresponding permeation of the body with that space, had been formalised into a spiritual practice in the Tantric tradition of Kashmir Shaivism several hundred years earlier, as a means by which the feeling of separation may be dissolved.

Suffice it to say that, formalised or not, the softening of the boundary between our self and all objects and others is a natural and inevitable consequence of the recognition of our true nature.

The more deeply we investigate the nature of our essential self, the less limitation we find. We find limited thoughts, feelings and sensations, but that which is aware of them, and within which they arise, does not share their limits, just as the space of a room does not share the limited qualities of the objects that exist within it or the walls that seem to contain it.

This liberation of our self from the confines within which it is normally contained may be experienced as a feeling of release or expansion, and may be accompanied by a great relaxation of the tension in the body and the agitation in the mind.

The feeling of expansion and the corresponding loss of the sense of separation may take place gradually, almost imperceptibly, over a period of time. Or it may take place suddenly and spontaneously.

We may be walking along a street or path and suddenly the sense of being solid, dense and located dissolves. We experience the world as a stream of perceptions and the body as a flow of sensations appearing in the openness of awareness. We are not a body walking through the world; the body and the world are flowing through us.

We continue to experience the world through the medium of the body, but the body has lost its separating power. The universe becomes our body.

* William Wordsworth, *Lines Composed a Few Miles above Tintern Abbey* (1798).

A SINGLE, SHARED REALITY

Einstein once remarked, 'Common sense is a series of prejudices that most people acquire by the age of eighteen'. Most of us have been conditioned to trust the evidence of common sense: a combination of perception and thought that fragments the unity of being into a multiplicity and diversity of discrete objects and selves, each with its own apparently separate and individual existence.

However, everyone has first-hand, direct knowledge of the underlying reality of the universe through the experiences of love and beauty. In the experience of love, we recognise our shared reality with all people and animals. In the experience of beauty, we recognise our shared reality with all objects and nature.

Imagine the space of my study, in Oxford, where I am now writing, and compare it with the space in which you are currently sitting as you read this book. They seem to be two separate and unique spaces, each with its own particular size, shape, location, and so on.

Now imagine that each of us were to remove all the objects from our room and even to dismantle the walls within which the space seems to be contained. What remains of the difference between our two rooms? Are they still separate? Have they united? Were they ever really separate to begin with? Were there really even two spaces to begin with?

Now do the same experiment with yourself. Imagine removing from yourself all the temporary, changing elements of your experience: thoughts, images, memories, feelings, sensations, perceptions, activities, relationships, and so on. What remains of yourself? Just formless, aware being.

Now do the same experiment in your imagination with someone you love. Remove, in your imagination, everything that is not essential to them. What remains? Formless, aware being. Are your being and their being still separate? Have you united? Were you ever really two separate beings to begin with?

Your shared being has simply been revealed, now that it is no longer obscured by the respective elements of your experience. That revelation of your shared being is the experience of love.

We can do the same thought experiment with someone we dislike or resent, either someone we know in person or someone we know of through the media. What we dislike is some aspect of their conditioned character, not their essential being or self.

Whether we like somebody or not is determined by the relationship between one character and another, between one set of conditioning and another, that is, the content of each of their thoughts, feelings, activities and relationships. The experience of love has nothing to do with whether we like or dislike a person's character. It is the recognition of our shared being. Divested of the conditioning that defines our character and dictates the way we think, feel, act and relate, we are all the same indivisible being.

The same is true of the vast majority of people whom we will never meet. The contents of my room in Oxford and your room at home will never interact, but nevertheless the space in which they appear is the *same* space. Likewise, although two characters may never meet, they still share their being. When we are moved by an image of a child in distress on the other side of the world, we are, without necessarily realising it, feeling their being as our own.

This also explains why we sometimes meet a person for the first time but feel we are reuniting with an old friend. We do not really meet them; we recognise them. There is something familiar about them and we feel at ease in their company. In this case, it is not necessary to know anything about them as a person to feel that, at the deepest level, we share our being.

In the experience of love, our shared being filters through the otherness of the apparent other. The name and form of the other ceases to conceal our shared being and becomes transparent to it. However, many long-term relationships end in conflict because the interaction of our personalities progressively obscures our shared being. We fall in love with someone's essence; we have to live with their personality.

When we first meet, we *feel* our shared essence. That is the experience of love. It is only later that we encounter each other's personality, that is, the layers of conditioning which subsequently veil our shared being. The word 'personality' comes from the Latin word *persona*, meaning 'mask', implying a disguise that covers our real face. Our personalities prevent us from 'seeing the original face' of our companion, that is, from feeling our shared being.

If we look at whatever conflicts may exist in our own life, and when we look around us at those that exist between individuals, communities and nations, it is tragic to realise that, at the deepest level, everybody already loves one another. That is, we all share our being.

Love *is* the recognition of our shared being. After all, when we love someone, do we not feel to a greater or lesser extent that everything that divides or separates us dissolves? In love, the other is not other. This is true of our relationship with animals as well as people.

In fact, we do not *share* being, as if being were an attribute of individual people. Ultimately, there are no individuals, no separate selves. There is just infinite, indivisible and utterly intimate being, which shines in each of us as the sense of 'being myself' or 'I am', before it is qualified by experience.

Love is not a relationship between two people; it is the *collapse* of relationship. It is the dissolution of everything that defines a person as a separate, independently existing entity, and the revelation of the being that we share with all others. It is the dawn of unity.

As Rumi said, 'Lovers don't finally meet somewhere; they're in each other all along'.*

THE SELF OF ALL SELVES

Love is unconditional. It does not depend on the attitudes, opinions, actions or behaviour of a person. It is simply the recognition that at the deepest level we share our being.

We are not required to like everybody, but we are called to love everybody. We are called to recognise that *their* being is *our* being, that we *share* our being, and to act and relate with them in a manner that is consistent with this understanding. Whether or not we *like* someone depends upon the extent to which our conditioning and theirs are in harmony, but there is no room for preferences in love.

Next time a loved one fails to treat us in the way that we would like to be treated, or says something unkind or disrespectful, we may become aware of the impulse to react emotionally and to retaliate on behalf of a hurt self. If we look for that hurt self, we never find it. We may find thoughts, feelings and actions that arise on behalf of a hurt self, but we never find the hurt self itself.

When we trace our way back through the layers of thought and feeling in search of our self, we find only the inherently peaceful and unconditionally

---

*Jelaluddin Rumi, 'The Minute I Heard My First Love Story' (1246), *The Essential Rumi*, translated by Coleman Barks (HarperOne, 2004).

fulfilled presence of awareness. The self finds or recognises itself, the self of all selves, the being of all beings.

The impulse to react or retaliate on behalf of a hurt self dissolves in this understanding. We may thank the other in our heart, if not to their face, for exposing in us the residues of the ego, and welcome the opportunity to deepen our conviction that we share our being with everyone, irrespective of what they say or do.

Whenever we think of, speak to or interact with another person, we should first feel in our heart that we share our being with them, and then allow our thoughts, words and actions to be informed by this felt understanding.

This single understanding would transform relationships between individuals, families, communities and nations. Imagine what our society would look like if not only people in general, but the politicians and leaders of our institutions in particular, understood and acted in accordance with this simple, universal principle. As Jacob Boehme said, 'If men would as fervently seek after love and righteousness as they do after opinions, there would be no strife on earth'. *

This does not imply that we lose the ability to recognise behaviour in ourself or others that does not come from the felt understanding of our shared being, or to respond appropriately in the face of such behaviour. On the contrary, we become better able to discern those attitudes and actions in ourself and in others that are not informed by the knowledge of our shared being, and we respond accordingly.

Shantananda Saraswati used to tell the story of an Indian teacher who was walking in the jungle with his disciples, discoursing with them on the subject of our shared being. At one point a tiger sprang out of the bushes and came bounding towards them; quick as a flash, the teacher leapt for safety at the top of the nearest tree.

When the danger had passed, his disciples confronted him, 'How come you were the first up the nearest tree, when only a few moments earlier you were telling us about the being we share with all people and all animals?' The teacher replied, 'I know that I share my being with the tiger, but the tiger doesn't yet know that he shares his being with me, and so I acted appropriately'.

*Jacob Boehme, *Of Regeneration*: VII: 169 (1622).

A response to a situation that is no longer mediated by the sense of separation will not give rise to conflict and hostility. This will give the situation the best possible chance of a fair and harmonious resolution for all parties.

In time, as the residues of the sense of separation are washed out of the mind and heart, there is an increase of empathy in our relationships and of compassion in our behaviour. We then become an instrument of love in whatever particular field or circumstance we find ourself.

MY HAPPINESS DOES NOT DEPEND ON YOU

This understanding has profound implications for every aspect of our lives, perhaps none more so than intimate relationships. If we seek such a friendship with the purpose of finding happiness or love, we are placing an impossible demand upon our future partner.

Such a relationship originates from need masquerading as love. If an intimate relationship is initiated for the purpose of putting an end to the sense of lack or the feeling of loneliness, the sense of lack that initiated the relationship will remain present in seed form underneath the initial euphoria and will later make itself known in the form of conflict.

To invest another person with the power to make us happy is to set them up for failure and ourself for disappointment. Sooner or later, usually after a honeymoon period that may last from a few weeks to a few years, our partner's behaviour will no longer conform to our expectations. Being unaware that the ensuing suffering is entirely our own activity, we will blame the other for it.

If only one person carries this projection, there is a possibility that the absence of reaction in their companion will defuse the situation and provide an opportunity for them to grow in understanding. However, one of the most common ways for an ego or apparently separate self to perpetuate itself is through conflict, so it is unlikely that such an approach will be successful, unless it is coupled with therapeutic intervention. If both parties carry this projection, the scene is set for inevitable conflict.

This is not a reason for not seeking intimate relationship. It is a reason for not *seeking happiness* in intimate relationship. Our desire for intimate relationship, or indeed any other object or circumstance, should come *from* happiness rather than as a means of acquiring it. The object, activity or relationship then becomes the medium through which peace and joy is communicated, shared and celebrated.

This is not a path of renunciation. It is a path of understanding and enjoyment. Nor do I mean to imply that it may not sometimes be legitimate to address unloving or unjust behaviour in a partner, as well as in ourself, if a relationship is to evolve in line with love and understanding.

Those who are already in a long-term relationship would do their relationship a great service by understanding that their companion can never fulfil their demand that they produce happiness or love for them and, as a result, withdrawing that expectation.

One of the kindest things we can say to our partner is, 'I love you, but my happiness is not dependent upon you'. It will relieve our friend of the impossible burden of producing love and happiness for us and will give the relationship the best possible chance of being truly loving and intimate.

FREEDOM FROM THE SEARCH

The understanding that peace and happiness cannot be given or taken away by external circumstances is one of the greatest discoveries a person can make, and it is often accompanied by a feeling of liberation and profound relaxation. We no longer need to constantly negotiate experience, resisting what is present and seeking what is not present, for the purpose of finding happiness.

This does not imply that we withdraw from life in any way. On the contrary, we simply cease expecting events and people to make us happy. We withdraw the impossible demand on our friends that they be a source of love, and from circumstances that they be a source of happiness. When we are able to experience people and circumstances as they are, without the layer of expectation and need through which our previous interactions with them were filtered, the universe will respond in a way that confirms its approval.

Nor does this understanding imply that we lead a life of passive resignation or cease responding to situations and taking appropriate action when necessary. We do not allow ourself, or those in our care, to be abused, nor are we silent in the face of injustice. One who is established in their true nature and living in harmony with the unfolding of the universe does not refrain from action, but their actions are not initiated by the anxieties, fears and desires that characterise the separate self or ego.

Rather, their actions are informed by qualities that emanate directly from the deepest part of our being, qualities that are shared by all people but in so many cases are temporarily obscured by layers of conditioning. When liberated from the demands of the person, our innate enthusiasm, kindness, clarity, compassion and sense of justice become the means by which eternal truths are expressed in response to temporary circumstances.

One in whom this understanding is alive may or may not make a conscious attempt to intervene in any particular situation. However, their presence and their response will, to a greater or lesser extent, restore balance and harmony, even if the effect of their intervention is not immediately apparent due to other elements in the situation beyond their control.

If our response comes from harmony with a situation rather than opposition to it, we align ourself with the totality and our action cannot help but be beneficial. Such action will always contribute to the unfolding of love and understanding in humanity. It is for this reason that Ramana Maharshi said, 'Realisation of the Self is the greatest help that can be rendered to humanity'.*

* *Talks with Ramana Maharshi: On Realizing Abiding Peace and Happiness*, 2nd ed. (Inner Directions Foundation, 2010).

CHAPTER NINETEEN

The All-Pervasive Spirit

*I have created perception in you only
in order to be the object of My perception.*

IBN ʿARABI

OUR SHARED BEING

As we explore the nature of our being, it begins to lose the limited qualities
that it derives from experience. It relinquishes the turbulence of thoughts,
the afflictive quality of emotions and the solidity of sensations, and is revealed
as peace and happiness.

As it loses its constraints, it becomes 'wider', more open, less bounded.
We begin to feel that we share our being with all other people and animals.
There is an increase in sensitivity, empathy and compassion. Its nature of
love reveals itself.

But why should we stop there? Why draw a boundary around all sentient
beings? After all, everything that is *exists*. As such, existence is the common
factor in *everything*, be that thing a person, a planet, a mountain, a body,
a thought, an atom, and so on.

The word 'existence' comes from two Latin words, *ex*, meaning 'out of'
or 'from', and *sistere*, meaning 'to stand', implying that something that exists
stands out. Stands out from what? From being.

Being is the shared background out of which everything emerges, in which it
exists and into which it vanishes. Being is, as such, that from which everyone and
everything borrows its apparently independent existence, just as all the characters
and objects in a movie borrow its reality, relatively speaking, from the screen.

However, just as no character or object on the screen actually stands out
from the screen with its own independent existence, but only seems to, likewise no person or thing actually stands out from the background of infinite
being with a status of its own.

We are not *parts* of infinite being, nor do we *emerge* from it as separate and independently existing entities. When we see a crowd of ten thousand people in a movie, the people do not divide the screen into separate parts, nor do they emerge out of the screen. The screen remains a single, homogeneous, undivided whole. The indivisible unity of the screen *appears* as a multiplicity and diversity of people.

Likewise, in reality, no person or thing emerges out of infinite being with its own discrete and independent existence, nor does the appearance of any person or thing divide infinite being into separate, individual parts. There are no separate parts.

Ultimately, there are no independently existing individual people or objects. There is no room for the finite in the infinite. The unity of being assumes the form of multiplicity and diversity without ever becoming anything other than itself.

For one who understands this, the world is evidence of the infinite nature of reality. It shines with its own reality. For one who does not understand this, the same world seems to be evidence of the discrete and independent experience of people and things. It is an apparent confirmation of a paradigm of separation. The world appears in accordance with the point of view we bring to it.

THE REVELATION OF BEAUTY

Our shared reality is not confined to people and animals. When we stand in awe in front of nature, become absorbed in a piece of music, are moved by the sight of an object or enjoy a delicious meal, the distinction between our self and the object dissolves. We experience the reality we share with that object. That is the experience of beauty!

The experience of beauty is an intervention of reality into our normal mode of perception, namely, the subject–object relationship. It is the cleansing of Blake's 'doors of perception'.* It is the apprehension of the poet Samuel Coleridge's 'One Life within us and abroad'.† The essential nature of our self and the reality of the object lose the dividing line that seems to define each

* 'If the doors of perception were cleansed everything would appear to man as it is, Infinite', William Blake, *The Marriage of Heaven and Hell* (c. 1790).
† Samuel Taylor Coleridge, *The Eolian Harp* (1828).

as a separate and discrete entity in its own right. And what was that dividing line made of? Thought!

In the experience of beauty, the name and form of the object cease to conceal our shared being and instead become transparent to it. They shine with it. When we experience beauty we are 'tasting' the reality that we share with the object. Or rather, infinite being, divested of its limitations, is tasting itself. It is aware of itself. That experience is timeless – it takes place in eternity – for in the absence of thought there is no sense of time.

The experience of beauty is in relation to objects and nature as the experience of love is to people and animals. It is the dissolution of the subject–object relationship through which our experience of reality is normally mediated, and the simultaneous revelation of our shared being. It is never the object itself that is beautiful. The so-called beautiful object possesses a particular quality that effects the collapse of the subject–object relationship, revealing its prior unity with the perceiver. In the experience of beauty, our shared being filters through the objectness of the apparent object, just as in the experience of love, our shared being shines through the otherness of the apparent other.

The word 'revelation' comes from the Latin *revelare*, meaning 'to lay bare'. As such, the experience of love or beauty is not a new or extraordinary experience that happens from time to time; it is the *revealing* or the *laying bare* of the nature of reality. It is the recognition that there is a single, infinite and indivisible whole or reality whose nature is spirit, awareness or being, from which all people, animals and things derive their apparently separate and independent existence. It is the revelation of the prior unity shared by everyone and everything.

If the understanding that we share our being is the source of the healing of conflicts between individuals, families, communities and nations, then the understanding that we share our being with all things must be the source of the restoration of the relationship between ourselves and nature or the environment.

This is the vision of the world that poets and artists try to restore. Art is to perception what philosophy is to thought. Poets gives us a window onto this world, artists a vision of this world. The English painter J. M. W. Turner was said to have been returning home from a day's painting on Hampstead Heath in North London when one of the local residents stopped him and asked to see the painting. The man surveyed the picture for some time and then remarked, 'I've lived here for forty years and have walked on Hampstead

Heath almost every day, but I have never seen a view like that'. To which Turner replied, 'No, but don't you wish you could?' The world is not what we see; it is the way we see.

We have become so accustomed to perceiving reality through the filter of our minds – the only way it is possible for us to experience anything – that we believe and feel that the fragmentation and separation that we experience in the world is a real quality *of* the world. Such is the intimate and participatory nature of the mind in the world that the world appears to conform with our belief about it. We do not think of the world because it exists; it seems to exist, as a multiplicity and diversity of discrete and independently existing objects and selves, because that is how we think of it.

William Blake imagines a conversation in which he tries to explain to his materialist friends the idea that there are no discrete, independently existing objects or selves, but rather a single, eternal, infinite and indivisible reality: '"What", it will be questioned, "When the sun rises, do you not see a round disk of fire somewhat like a guinea?" Oh no, no, I see an innumerable company of the heavenly host crying, "Holy, Holy, Holy, is the Lord God Almighty".'*

OBJECTS BORN, NOT MADE

In 1975, I was fifteen years old and had an experience which was to change the course of my life. Michael Cardew, one of the founding fathers of the British studio pottery movement, had a retrospective exhibition at the Camden Arts Centre in London to celebrate his seventy-fifth birthday. I knew of Michael through his wife, Mariel, who attended The Study Society at Colet House where I had just been introduced to the non-dual understanding, and I visited the exhibition at her suggestion.

Michael's pots were raw, energetic and powerful. They seemed to me more like brief moments of condensed music than physical objects. It felt as if they were fluid, arrested only by the act of perception, as if my senses were apprehending the energies of the universe and conferring upon them a temporary, static form. However, I was not observing them from a fixed point.

---

*'A Vision of the Last Judgment' (c. 1810), *Selected Poems from William Blake*, edited by P. H. Butter (Everyman, 1982).

I too was part of the indivisible flux of energies out of which the observer and the observed condensed in a reciprocal and mutually sustaining relationship.

Little did I know at the time that this confrontation was to put an end to my incipient desire to study medicine, or that five years later I would spend the last two years of Michael's life living and working with him at his pottery in Cornwall. Suffice it to say that I left with a simple desire, 'I want to learn to make pots like that'.

At the time I could not have known that such objects are 'born, not made'. Michael's pottery was more laboratory than studio, where the energies of nature were harnessed and condensed. One did not make things; one participated in their emergence. And should one ever forget this, one could be certain that Michael's anger would re-establish the balance.

On one such occasion, after being at Wenford Bridge for about six months, I had been making bowls all day and was beginning to feel that I was gaining some mastery over the medium. Michael came into the workshop at one end and made his way slowly through the long, narrow room, once used as a skittle alley, attached to the former inn which he and Mariel had converted into their home and the pottery. Michael surveyed the shelves of bowls for an alarmingly long period of time and, turning to me with a withering expression on his face, exclaimed, 'You haven't begun to take that shape into yourself'. And with no further discussion he left.

It was the first time that I was to experience the restorative power of impersonal anger. Such outbursts were not infrequent, and no explanation was ever offered. One was expected to take the medicine and make the necessary changes. It was in this way that I gradually came to understand that the making of a good pot involved a kind of sacrifice. How naïve of me to have imagined that the price of beauty was anything less than oneself.

Later on, whenever I found myself in a foreign city, I would spend hours in the ceramics department of the national or archaeological museum. Looking at the pots there, I would often have the feeling of experiencing them from the inside, as if I knew what it was like to be that object. I felt its body as my own body. This capacity was no doubt partly due to a natural affinity, but it had also been refined over the many years I had spent making such objects.

It was as if my own understanding of the materials and processes that are gathered together in the making of a bowl had given me access to the inner life of the object I was contemplating. Over the years, I noticed that this capacity extended beyond my chosen medium of ceramics and included, to a greater or lesser degree, other art forms, such as painting, music, sculpture, architecture and dance.

The Greek philosopher Plotinus referred to this when he said, 'In this state of absorbed contemplation, there is no longer any question of holding an object in view; the vision is such that seeing and seen are one; object and act of vision have become identical'.*

The German philosopher Arthur Schopenhauer referred to the same experience when he said, 'Aesthetic pleasure in the beautiful consists, to a large extent, in the fact that, when we enter the state of pure contemplation, we are raised for the moment above all willing, above all desires and cares; we are, so to speak, rid of ourselves'.†

THE TASTE OF NATURE'S ETERNITY

Everyone experiences this collapse of the subject–object relationship many times in their lives, although it is not always recognised as such. In fact, when we seek an experience, we invariably do so not for the sake of the experience itself but for its capacity to bring to an end the subject–object relationship, and the inevitable feeling of separation that attends it, thereby giving us a taste of the unity of being.

In sexual intimacy, all one's disparate energies are gathered together in the intensity of the moment, suspending the thinking process which habitually divides the intimacy of experience into the subject–object relationship, and through which the apparently separate self escapes the now. There is just the moment, no self and no other, no body and no world, no lover and no beloved. Not even a moment, for without reference to thought, there is no experience of time. We are taken to eternity.

For the apparently separate self, this collapse of the distinction between itself and the other feels like a death. Of course, in reality, an illusion cannot die.

---

*Plotinus, *The Enneads* v.1–8.
† Arthur Schopenhauer, *The World as Will and Representation*, Vol. 1, Sect. 68 (1819).

It simply ceases to veil its reality. However, the ego does not know this. Thus, what it experiences as death is, in reality, the shining forth of our shared being. It is the experience of love. This is why love and death are so closely related in art and literature.

It is for this reason that the poet Kathleen Raine wrote, in 'Woman to Lover', 'I am the way to die'.* Little does the separate self realise that in all of its desires, and perhaps especially in its desire for sexual intimacy, all that it is really seeking is to bring itself to an end, like the moth that seeks to unite with the flame.

When the separate self is reconstituted after its dissolution in eternity, it emerges 'trailing clouds of glory',† still shimmering with peace and joy, which, at least until it fades, it will bestow on everything and everyone with whom it comes in contact. It is the experience to which writer W. B. Yeats referred when he said, 'I felt that I was blessèd and could bless'.‡

Many people enjoy walking in the countryside because, in the absence of any sense of separation in nature, they access their shared being, which is prior to the arising of ego. For the same reason, many people love to live with animals because they model the quality of just being, wordlessly awakening the same being in us through sympathetic resonance.

For others food may be a portal into their true nature, although it is usually not recognised as such, not least because it is more often appropriated by the ego to satiate its voracious sense of lack. Little do we realise that, when eating a delicious meal or savouring a fine wine, we are literally tasting our self. Stephen Mitchell's rendition of Rainer Maria Rilke's *Sonnets to Orpheus* illustrates how just the taste of an apple has the power to divest reality of the limitations that the mind confers upon it, revealing its nature of beauty.

> What miracle is happening in your mouth?
> Instead of words, discoveries flow out
> from the ripe flesh, astonished to be free.

---

*Kathleen Raine, *Collected Poems*, Counterpoint Press (2001).
† William Wordsworth, 'Intimations of Immortality from Recollections of Early Childhood', *Poems, in Two Volumes* (1801).
‡ W. B. Yeats, 'Vacillation', Verse IV.

Dare to say what 'apple' truly is.
This sweetness that feels thick, dark, dense at first;
then, exquisitely lifted in your taste,

grows clarified, awake and luminous,
double-meaninged, sunny, earthy, real –
Oh knowledge, pleasure – inexhaustible.*

In many ancient cultures, aesthetic experience was considered sacred. In these cultures, the making and drinking of tea, walking in the landscape, the playing of a musical instrument, sharing a meal, the raising of children, the making of a home, in fact every moment of embodied experience, was considered an opportunity, even an invitation, to merge with the divine.

We may place flowers in our home, a painting on the wall, a jar on a shelf or a bowl on the table. In doing so, we intuitively recognise the power of certain objects to solicit the mind, to invite it away from its habitual discursive patterns and introduce a pause in which its background may be revealed. In a glance at a photo of a loved one on the mantelpiece, we are taken first to the person and then to the love we share. Our shared being shines.

* * *

Sensory experience is, for many people, the primary portal through which they briefly taste their innate joy. As William Blake observed, the five senses are 'the chief inlets of Soul in this age'.† That is, sense perception is the means by which the mind briefly returns from its adventure in time to the immediacy of the now. Without the filter of thought and feeling that characterises our normal experience, the distance between our self and our current experience subsides, and the joy that is the very nature of our being shines forth.

In the experience of enjoyment, we, awareness, are tasting the innate joy of our own being. This understanding is concealed in common parlance in a phrase such as, 'I enjoyed myself at the party last night'. The object, event

---

* Rainer Maria Rilke, *The Sonnets to Orpheus* 1, 13, translated by Stephen Mitchell (Vintage, 2009).
† William Blake, *The Marriage of Heaven and Hell* (c. 1790).

or person was simply the context in which this enjoyment was invited, courted and revealed. It was not the party we enjoyed; it was our self that we enjoyed, that is, our self was enjoying itself. Awareness was tasting or knowing its own being. The party was a gathering of the senses on the threshold of the divine.

Art is a formalisation of this process. The ultimate purpose of art is to provide access to the sacred dimension of life, without the need for renunciation or asceticism, but through the very energies of life itself. As the writer D. H. Lawrence observed, 'Art is a form of supremely delicate awareness... meaning at-oneness, the state of being at one with the object'.*

Nowhere, to my knowledge, is this understanding stated more clearly than by the painter Paul Cézanne: 'Everything vanishes, falls apart, doesn't it? Nature is always the same but nothing in her that appears to us lasts. Our art must render the thrill of her permanence, along with her elements, the appearance of all her changes. It must give us a taste of nature's Eternity.'†

All we know of the world are perceptions, and perceptions are intermittent. They fall apart, vanish. And yet in spite of the fact that everything we know about the universe is constantly changing, we recognise that there is something that persists through it all that is greater than our self as a person and beyond the limits of the finite mind through which we perceive it. At the same time, we realise that we too emanate from the universe and that whatever limitations our finite mind superimposes on it, its essence is the same as our own.

This intuition of the unlimited nature of our being and its interconnection with all things is always accompanied by joy, 'the thrill of her permanence'. It restores our original innocence and freedom. The purpose of art, according to Cézanne, is to use the changing elements of experience – sights in his case, sounds in the case of musicians, tastes for cooks, textures for sculptors, words for writers and poets, and so on – and bring them together in such a way that they take us, not intellectually but experientially, to this ever-present reality. They give us a taste of nature's eternity.

---

*D. H. Lawrence, 'Making Pictures', *The Creative Process: A Symposium*, Brewster Ghiselin Ed. (University of California Press, 1985).
† J. Gasquet, *Cézanne* (1926), as translated in: John Rewald, 'Catalogue', *Cézanne: The Late Work* (1977).

RESTORING THE SACRED

There are many other occasions when, in the natural course of our everyday life, a window opens up in the flow of experience, allowing the qualities that are inherent in our true nature to flow into the situation, informing it with its innate intelligence. Many people report that the experience of bereavement is often accompanied by a quiet joy. In this case, the immensity of the loss brings their life, as they know it, to an end. The normal filter of thoughts and feelings through which experience is filtered collapses, and in that moment their true nature shines.

In other cases, a person's first glimpse of their true nature is sometimes preceded by a period of great sorrow or despair. In the hopelessness that ensues, all future possibilities are removed and, with nowhere to go, one is brought back to the sanctity of the now. Such experiences bring the activity of the ego, which is always invested in future happiness, to an end and thus provide an opportunity to sink into the vertical dimension of our being. However, through lack of guidance, such invitations are often missed and, as a result, simply compound our suffering.

For others it may be an illness, a failed relationship, the loss of financial security, the onset of old age or the imminence of death. Unlike normal circumstances, in which a person usually feels that they can intervene in order to effect the change that they believe is required for their happiness, experiences such as these, where the intensity of feeling is such that we find ourself powerless in the face of it, overshadow any such attempt to negotiate.

In the spontaneous surrender that ensues, we find ourself open without resistance to our current experience. The layer of personal psychology, built almost entirely of resisting, holding on and seeking, which constitutes the activity of the separate self or ego, has dissolved. No longer able to muster the strength to resist, we find ourself at one with the experience and, as a result, our innate peace emerges from the background.

The peace was, of course, present in us all along but was veiled, not by the sorrow, the despair or the loss but by the activity of resisting, holding on and seeking. This is the quiet joy that can emerge even in the depths of suffering. It is referred to as *ananda* in the Vedantic tradition and as 'the peace that passeth understanding' in the Christian tradition. It is the peace that is prior to and independent of the content of the experience.

In an emergency, the situation is sometimes so demanding that we do not have time to refer to the thought processes with which we would normally respond to such an event. Our response to the situation is, as a result, not mediated through a layer of past conditioning. It comes spontaneously, as a direct response in the moment. This allows the person to draw on a source of strength that lies behind their conditioned thoughts and feelings, in the very heart of themselves, and accounts for acts of courage and compassion that often extend far beyond a person's normal capabilities.

When the emergency is over, people will often praise the one who acted in this way. However, the person will not have any sense of having undertaken or achieved anything remarkable. They will know intuitively that their actions came not from themselves as a person but from a deeper, impersonal source within them, and therefore they will not lay claim to them.

Intense fear is another experience that brings one abruptly into the now and may thus be a natural portal to one's true nature. In a culture where the egoic activity of seeking and resisting, and the inevitable suffering and conflict that attend it, dominate both individuals and institutions, the possibility of finding a means whereby one may access the awareness that lies behind the mind and thus transcend the ego is still relatively rare, although this is beginning to change. However, in the absence of such guidance, the innate intelligence that is the essence of each person's mind will find its own way of making its presence felt.

It may be felt as a person's yearning for happiness or love, a devotee's longing for God, a scientist's desire for understanding or an artist's love of beauty. Or it may find more extreme ways of infiltrating a person's experience. When a young man launches himself from a great height with only an elastic cord tied around his feet, he is, probably without realising it, putting himself through a self-ordained initiation rite in which he faces and overcomes the fear of death. As he propels himself into an experience that, on account of its intensity, brings him into the immediacy of the now, he is divested of the limitations of time – memories, fears, anger, sorrow, resentment, hope, and so on – and tastes his innate freedom.

Another may train for years at a sport, always pushing the edge of her endurance and capacity, in order to expand beyond the limits which she intuitively knows do not define her. To expand beyond our limitations is like a death for the one who is identified with them; for others, it is a rebirth. Divested of the constraints that thought imposes upon her self, she finds herself in the zone, at one with the flow of the universe, and able to perform at a level well beyond her normal capacity.

Others may marvel at what appear to be super-human accomplishments. Indeed, they are super-human, in the sense that they are inspired by, and an expression of, an aspect of ourself that is prior to our human limitations. Even as a spectator one partakes of this moment of transcendence, and it is for this reason that we confer god-like status on highly skilled athletes.

And there are quieter ways of inviting our true nature to reveal itself. Consider, for instance, the poet who sits in front of a piece of paper, the mind open and receptive, inviting that which lies behind the mind to assume a form within the mind. As Rilke wrote, 'I love the dark hours of my being. My mind deepens into them.' *

In his book *Pioneer Pottery*, Michael Cardew said, referring to the capacity of a pot to draw the mind into its source, 'Its presence will fill the gaps between sips of tea or coffee at those moments when the mind, not yet focused on activity, is still in an open and receptive state; and it will minister quietly to the background of consciousness with a friendly warmth, even perhaps on some occasions with a kind of consolation'.†

For others it may take place unsolicited in the natural pause after the ending of one activity and before the mind reaches for the next. Or simply walking in nature, surrendering one's body to its immensity.

When we are at home or in our workplace, the familiarity of the environment is such that many routine activities can be undertaken without our needing to attend to or focus on them. With nothing particular to interest or engage the mind, we are free to wander into the past or future seeking relief from the tedium of the now. However, when we travel, the sights, sounds, tastes, textures and smells that we encounter are often sufficiently unfamiliar to fascinate us and, as a result, command our attention. The mind returns to the now from

---

*Rainer Maria Rilke, Untitled ('I Love the Dark Hours of My Being'), *The Book of Hours: Love Poems to God*, translated by Anita Barrows and Joanna Macy (Riverhead, 1997).
† Michael Cardew, *Pioneer Pottery* (The American Ceramic Society, 2002).

its adventure in time. The happiness we feel on this occasion does not rise on account of our new environment; it is the taste of our true nature.

A good storyteller will eke out a joke, gradually winding up his listeners into a state of heightened expectation, knowing that the greater the tension, the deeper the feeling of relief upon hearing the punchline. And the listener will readily participate in this heightened state of anticipation for the pleasure of having it come to an end in the moment of understanding. Before the joke has come to an end, the understanding has not yet taken place. By the time the laughter begins, the understanding has *already* taken place.

In the timeless moment between the end of the joke and the beginning of the laughter, understanding occurs. That which 'stands under' the mind emerges from obscurity beneath the mind. The smile or laughter that follows is the relaxation of the body in response to this plunge into our true nature. Indeed, every time someone smiles at us, we receive a blessing in which the light of being shines on us. Every time we smile at someone, we bestow that blessing on them.

Suffice it to say that there are innumerable ways, some effortless and spontaneous, others cultivated, whereby the obscuring activity of the mind may be dissolved and, as a result, its essence revealed – 'hints of the beloved', as they say in the Sufi tradition. In fact, I would suggest that the mind is always tending towards its source, the heart always longing for its home, and that almost all people are most of the time, whether they realise it or not, engaged in this attempt to return to their true nature.

Of course, this is said from the perspective of an individual mind. In reality, it is unlimited awareness that, identifying itself with, or losing itself in, the content of experience seems to have become localised and limited. In the form of this apparently limited mind or self, awareness is always attempting to divest itself of this limitation and return to its natural condition. It is for this reason that an individual mind or self constantly feels the gravitational pull of its true nature in the form of its search for happiness, truth, love or beauty.

Whether or not the finite mind seeks to alleviate the suffering that is inherent in its own limited condition through the acquisition of objects, substances, activities, circumstances and relationships, or by going directly to its essence by means of meditation, self-enquiry or prayer, depends upon its maturity.

YOU ARE THE HAPPINESS YOU SEEK

But either way, the mind is destined sooner or later to be dissolved in its essence. Just as water evaporates from the ocean, forms into clouds, drifts over the earth, falls in rain, turns into wine, is shed in tears, gathers into rivers and returns to the ocean, continually changing its name and form but never changing its essence, so the apparent individual, feeling itself to be separate from the whole, embarks on a great journey, passes through many adventures, assumes many guises and eventually returns to its original nature, without ever actually having ceased to be as such.

Each of the examples above indicate some of the many instances during our lives when our customary thought processes are interrupted and, as a result, the peace and joy of our true nature, which lies just behind the mind, emerges naturally and effortlessly into the foreground of our experience.

Although the event which precedes the emergence of our innate peace and joy differs in each case, the effect it has on us is the same: surrender. A wise person is one who does not wait for circumstances or events to initiate this surrender. They simply make it their moment-by-moment attitude.

THE PEACE OF DEEP SLEEP

One last example will illustrate that, concealed within our ordinary experience, there lie numerous traces of the divine. Many people believe that deep sleep is the absence of awareness. The reason for this is that awareness is considered dependent upon the content of experience. No experience, no awareness.

However, deep sleep is not the absence of awareness; it is the awareness of absence. When we fall asleep at night, the mind lets go of all objective experience naturally and effortlessly, leaving its essence, pure awareness, all alone, resting in its own being. That is the experience of peace.

When my son was very young, he would sometimes get upset. During these times there was nothing his mother, Caroline, or I could do to console him, and he would often say, 'I just want to go to sleep'. He had experienced the peace of his true nature in deep sleep on numerous occasions, as we all do, and now, in the face of his distress, he instinctively knew how to find his way back there. It was for the same reason that Ramana Maharshi once said, 'Meditation is like falling asleep whilst remaining awake'.

After a period of deep sleep, the dreaming and waking states emerge again, but nothing happens to the presence of awareness which shone there all along. Layers of experience are simply added to it: images and thoughts in the dream state, to which sensations, perceptions, activities and relationships are added in the waking state. However, just as the transparency of a screen seems to be veiled when a movie begins, so the peace and joy that is the nature of pure awareness seems to be obscured when objective experience resumes.

In this case, all one need do is to invite the mind gently back to its source, the abode of peace and happiness, the presence of awareness. For one who has been exploring these matters for some time and is accustomed to returning again and again from the adventure of experience to the peace of their true nature, the first taste of suffering that accompanies this forgetting will be sufficient to initiate the return home, without the need for a method or practice.

However, for one in whom this habit is not yet established, the mind may need to be coaxed away from its fascination with and reliance upon the content of experience. For such a mind, a question such as, 'Am I aware?', 'What is it that knows or is aware of my experience?', 'Who am I?', 'What is it that can never be removed from me?' or 'What element of my experience is always with me?' will suffice.

Each time we disengage from the content of experience and return to our true nature of pure awareness that lies in the background, we are eroding the power of objective experience to take us away from our self. In time, less and less effort is needed and less and less time required. We begin to be established in the peace and happiness of our true nature.

The greatest discovery one can make in life is to find one's way back to one's innate peace and joy, without the need for circumstances to align themselves with our preconceived ideas, and without having to fall asleep.

An Invitation

Pour yourself out like a fountain.
Flow into the knowledge that what you are seeking
finishes often at the start, and, with ending, begins.

RAINER MARIA RILKE

There are essentially two models for civilisation. The first is one in which the ideas and attitudes of individuals are informed by an understanding of their relationship to the whole, and their activities and relationships are the means by which this understanding is expressed in society.

The second model is one in which individuals overlook their relationship to the whole and, as a result, believe and feel themselves to be discrete, independently existing entities. This is a paradigm of separation that inevitably leads to unhappiness on the inside, conflict on the outside between individuals, communities and nations, and the exploitation and degradation of the earth.

History has repeatedly shown that a civilisation in which individuals neglect their relationship with the whole will collapse. Our own civilisation is showing all the signs of this disintegration but has as yet failed to embrace the understanding required to remedy it. We are like a patient who has been diagnosed with a terminal illness but refuses to take the medicine. We have alienated ourselves from the whole by believing ourselves to be separate parts.

THREE ESSENTIAL QUESTIONS

The non-dual understanding that lies at the origin of all the great religious, spiritual and philosophical traditions is formulated in response to three existential questions: 'How may we find lasting peace and happiness?', 'What is the nature of reality?' and 'How should we live?'

The first question, 'How may we find lasting peace and happiness?', relates to our inner life, and to this the non-dual understanding replies, 'Peace and happiness is the very nature of your being'.

We arrive at this understanding by separating our self from everything that is not essential to us: our thoughts, images, feelings, sensations, perceptions, activities and relationships. All that remains is our essential, irreducible being. Divested of everything with which we previously defined our self, we find our self empty, silent and at peace.

The second question, 'What is the nature of reality?', relates to our outer life, our relationship with all people, animals and our environment. In response to this the non-dual understanding suggests, 'We share our being with everyone and everything'. That is, there is a single, infinite and indivisible reality from which everyone and everything derives its apparently independent existence.

As we sink more and more deeply into our being, it loses its agitation on the inside and, at the same time, its limitations on the outside. The being that we essentially are is the same being that everyone and everything essentially is.

Being is infinite and indivisible. Previously the multiplicity and diversity of people, animals and things veiled their shared reality. Now they lose their veiling power and become transparent to it.

If we understand these two aspects of our self and lead a life, to the best of our ability, in a way that is consistent with their implications, no other spiritual instruction or practice is necessary.

If we understand that happiness is the very nature of our being, we cease expecting or demanding that other people and the world provide it. Our happiness is no longer a hostage to circumstance. We cease using the world to serve our happiness and instead use our happiness to serve the world.

If we understand and feel that we share our being with all people, animals and things, no further code of ethics or morality is required. That understanding is the foundation of all ethical behaviour.

The response to the third question, 'How should we live?', is an inevitable consequence of this understanding. When asked the same question,

St. Augustine replied, 'Love, and do whatever you want'. That is, recognise and feel the prior unity from which everyone and everything derives its apparently independent existence, and act in a manner that expresses and communicates this understanding in the world.

There is almost no field of human endeavour in which it is not possible to allow this understanding to inform our thoughts and feelings and to express itself in our activities and relationships.

All the qualities that we most admire in a human being are those that express, or are informed by, the recognition that the nature of our being is happiness and that we share our being with everyone and everything.

Qualities such as kindness, humility, dignity, compassion, respect, generosity, courage, integrity, humour and creativity all arise from the recognition or intuition that beneath our differences we share our being. Such qualities are expressions of the divine in a human being.

For one in whom this understanding is alive, the unity of being increasingly outshines the apparent multiplicity and diversity of people, animals and things. Everything becomes transparent to and shines with its reality.

KNOW THYSELF

The unity of being is refracted through the faculties of thought and perception and appears, as a result, as a multiplicity and diversity of objects and selves. If we take the evidence of sense perception and the categorising faculty of thought at face value, and we consider everyone and everything a discrete entity with its own separate and independent existence, then suffering, conflict and destruction are inevitable.

Individuals pay for this paradigm with their happiness; humanity is paying for it with its sanity. If pursued unchecked, it must eventually lead to a catastrophic outcome.

If, instead, we take the evidence of reason and experience, we see through the illusory appearance of separation to the single, infinite and indivisible reality that underlies it and of which it is an expression.

Every thought or feeling that we entertain, and every action or relationship in which we engage, can be traced back to one of these two possible perspectives. Our life as an individual and the destiny of our civilisation as a whole depend upon which of these two perspectives we subscribe to.

It is in response to the paradigm of fragmentation and separation that the founders of all the great religious and spiritual traditions have, in numerous different ways, implored humanity to awaken to a single understanding: happiness is the nature of our being, and we share our being with everyone and everything.

All that is necessary is to understand this, feel this and lead a life, to the best of our ability, in a way that is consistent with it, engaging in activities and relationships that, in one way or another, communicate and celebrate it.

We cannot know the nature of the universe directly, because the instrument through which we perceive and explore it, namely the mind, imposes its own limitations on everything that it knows. We cannot see white snow through orange-tinted glasses.

However, we *can* know our self, because we have direct, unmediated knowledge of our self before it is filtered through the limitations of thought and perception. Divested of the limitations that our self acquires from thought and perception, we know our self simply as infinite, impersonal, self-aware being.

Whatever the universe is, we as apparent individuals emerge from it. Therefore, whatever we essentially are must be the reality of the universe from which we seem to emerge, just as the nature of the wave must be identical to that of the ocean.

It is from this observation that the central tenet of all the great religious and spiritual traditions is derived: in Christianity, 'I and my Father are one'; in Hinduism, 'Atman and Brahman are identical'; in Buddhism, 'Nirvana and samsara are one' and 'Form is emptiness and emptiness also is form'; and in Sufism, 'Whosoever knows their self knows their Lord'. That is, the awareness that is the essential nature of our self is the ultimate reality of the universe.

Thus, self-knowledge is not only the direct path to peace and happiness; it is also the pre-requisite for understanding the nature of the universe. The reason why scientists have yet to discover the nature of the universe, in spite of searching for it for over two thousand years, is that they have yet to recognise the nature of their own minds.

If we make a deep investigation into the nature of our self, we find only infinite, impersonal, self-aware being. It finds and knows itself. From a human perspective these qualities, if we can refer to them as qualities, are felt as peace and happiness in relation to our inner experience, and as love and beauty in relation to all people, animals and objects. They are the very fabric of reality.

In other words, the universe is a manifestation of joy, love and beauty. If this seems not to be the case, it is only because we believe ourself to be temporary, finite and separate, and view the universe through the limitations of this filter.

For this reason, the words *Know Thyself*, which stood, two and a half thousand years ago, as an invitation to humanity at the dawn of Western civilisation, now stand as a prayer to our world civilisation as a whole.

The knowing of our own being is the means by which our innate peace and happiness may be restored. It is the means by which tolerance, compassion, cooperation and harmony may be established between all peoples. And it is the foundation on which depends the reparation of our relationship with nature.

To know the nature of one's self is the great understanding upon which any true civilisation must be founded.

QUOTATION SOURCES

EPIGRAPH
J. Krishnamurti, from the essay 'Creative Happiness'

INTRODUCTION
T. S. Eliot, 'Little Gidding', *Four Quartets* (Harcourt, 1941)

CHAPTER ONE
Aristotle, *Nicomachean Ethics*, Book 1, Section 7

CHAPTER TWO
Ramana Maharshi, *Who Am I?* (Sri Ramanasramam, 2008; orig. 1923)

CHAPTER THREE
Herman Hesse, *Wandering* (Farrar, Straus, and Giroux, 1972)

CHAPTER FOUR
Attributed to the sixteenth-century Zen patriarch Ikkyu, source unknown

CHAPTER FIVE
Attributed to the thirteenth-century German Christian mystic Meister Eckhart, source unknown

CHAPTER SIX
Frances Nuttall, 'The Prayer of the Chalice' (1962)

CHAPTER SEVEN
Alice Meynell, 'To the Beloved', *The Poems of Alice Meynell: Complete Edition* (McClelland and Stewart, 1923)

CHAPTER EIGHT
Plotinus, *The Enneads* VI.9.11.

CHAPTER NINE
Catherine of Siena, 'Consumed in Grace', *Love Poems from God*, translated by Daniel Ladinsky (Penguin Compass, 2002)

CHAPTER TEN
Li Po, 'Zazen on Ching-t'ing Mountain', *Crossing the Yellow River: Three Hundred Poems from the Chinese*, translated by Sam Hamill (BOA Editions Ltd., 2000)

CHAPTER ELEVEN
Awhad al-din Balyani, *Know Yourself*, translated by Cecilia Twinch (Beshara Publications, 2011)

CHAPTER TWELVE
Jelaluddin Rumi, 'An Empty Garlic', *The Essential Rumi*, translated by Coleman Barks (HarperOne, 2004)

CHAPTER THIRTEEN
Lao Tzu, Tao Te Ching, Chapter 26, as translated by Stephen Mitchell (Harper Perennial, 1994)

CHAPTER FOURTEEN
Anandamayi Ma, *Life and Teaching of Sri Anandamayi Ma*, edited by Dr. Alexander Lipsky (Motilal Banarsidass, 1977)

CHAPTER FIFTEEN
Leo Tolstoy, *A Calendar of Wisdom: Daily Thoughts to Nourish the Soul Written and Selected from the World's Sacred Texts*, translated by Peter Sekirin (Scribner, 1997)

CHAPTER SIXTEEN
Lao Tzu, Tao Te Ching, Chapter 47, as translated by Stephen Mitchell (Harper Perennial, 1994)

CHAPTER SEVENTEEN
Albert Camus, from the essay 'Return to Tipasa', *Personal Writings*, translated by Ellen Conroy Kennedy and Justin O'Brien (Vintage, 2020)

CHAPTER EIGHTEEN
Jesus, Gospel of Thomas, Saying 3

CHAPTER NINETEEN
'Listen, O Dearly Beloved', based on a translation of Muhyiddin Ibn 'Arabi, 'The Theophany of Perfection' in Henri Corbin, *Alone with the Alone: Creative Imagination in the Sufism of Ibn 'Arabi* (Routledge, 2007)

CONCLUSION
Rainer Maria Rilke, 'Want the Change', *In Praise of Mortality*, translated by Anita Barrows and Joanna Macy (Riverhead, 2005)

www.rupertspira.com